Broadway Christian C
Our Hopes Our Dreams A
Bauer, Gary L.

P9-DBT-479

0000   2993

Our Hopes

Our Dreams

A Vision for *America*

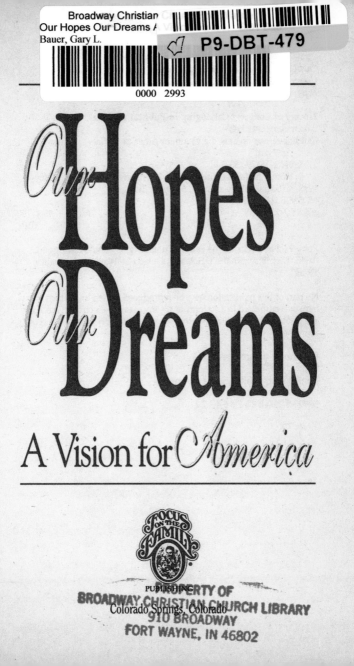

PUBLISHING
Colorado Springs, Colorado

PROPERTY OF
BROADWAY CHRISTIAN CHURCH LIBRARY
910 BROADWAY
FORT WAYNE, IN 46802

OUR HOPES, OUR DREAMS
Copyright © 1996 by Gary L. Bauer. All rights reserved. International
copyright secured.

Library of Congress Cataloging-in-Publication Data
Bauer, Gary Lee, 1946–
Our hopes, our dreams : a vision for America / Gary L. Bauer.
    p. cm.
  ISBN 1-56179-433-3
   1. Family policy—United States. 2. United States—Social policy—
1993- 3. Social values—United States. I. Title.
HQ536.B324 1996
306.85'0973—dc20
                                        95-49790
                                          CIP

Published by Focus on the Family Publishing, Colorado Springs, CO
80995. Distributed in the U.S.A. and Canada by Word Books, Dallas,
Texas.

No part of this publication may be reproduced, stored in a retrieval system, or transmitted in any form or by any means—electronic, mechani-
cal, photocopy, recording, or otherwise—without prior permission of the
publisher.

Front cover design: Brad Lind

Printed in the United States of America

96 97 98 99/10 9 8 7 6 5 4 3 2 1

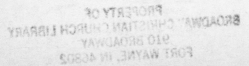
PROPERTY OF
BROADWAY CHRISTIAN CHURCH LIBRARY
910 BROADWAY
FORT WAYNE, IN 46802

Our Hopes, Our Dreams is dedicated to my loving wife, Carol, and to our children, Elyse, Sarah, and Zachary. It is my sincerest hope for all of America's children, both those present and those yet to come, that the ideals expressed in these pages will move closer to reality with each passing day. It is my fervent prayer that all of us responsible adults will rededicate ourselves to building a world where family, faith, and freedom are the living legacy to which every nation aspires and into which every child is born.

This book is also written in honor of a great American, Edwin Prince (1931–1995). Over the years, Ed was my faithful friend and thoughtful mentor, as well as a devoted brother in Christ. He and his wonderful family are real-life examples of what the American Dream is all about.

Contents

Renewing America

I was going to be interviewed by Dan Rather, the *CBS Evening News* anchor. He had come to Washington, D.C., to ask me about the movement of which I'm a part. As I approached the beautiful, historic Willard Hotel on Pennsylvania Avenue, near the White House, where we would meet, I thought back over the past week leading up to this face-to-face session with Rather.

A CBS camera crew had followed me and my family around for a few days, and a correspondent had interviewed us in our home. It was awkward at first, but we had gradually gotten used to the bright television lights, the electrical cables seemingly strewn everywhere, and the constant presence of strangers in our house and even in our car. Everywhere we went, they were sure to go. We tried to be pleasant and cooperative even though we felt a little like specimens under a magnifying glass. My younger children actually found the whole experience quite exciting.

Among the events the CBS team captured on film was a ceremony in which my daughter Sarah and others at her public high school took a pledge to remain sexually abstinent until marriage. We were pleased that the network was making note of our efforts to live out our ideals, but we had no little apprehension about how CBS News would "spin" the Bauers.

What am I, without the spin? A conservative in political outlook, a Christian by faith—in short, what millions of Americans are. That seems simple to me, but many in the media cannot resist stereotyping those who promote traditional values. The *Los Angeles Times* and *Wall Street Journal*, for example, referred to me as a "prominent social conservative."

The *Boston Globe* labeled me a "conservative activist."

The *Washington Post* said I was a "leading figure of the religious right."

Rolling Stone, in its characteristic style, called me a "values guru."

U.S. News & World Report took the prize by dubbing me a "fundamentalist firebrand."

The news media like such pithy, simple labels, because they usually try to explain complex issues in short, simple stories. But as I drew near the room where I would be meeting with Dan Rather that day in July 1995, I wondered, *Might I get the chance this time to give a fuller explanation of what our movement is all about? Can I convey in a relatively few words what America would look like if our dreams came true?*

Rather and I were scheduled to spend several hours one on one. The interview progressed in a fairly routine manner under the hot glare of the television lights until he posed a question I will not soon forget. "What do you want for America?" he asked. It wasn't a trick question at all. Instead, it was the chance I had been hoping for to speak from the heart about what inspires the movement in which I'm happy to play a role.

My organization, Family Research Council (FRC), has been in Washington nearly 15 years. Before coming to FRC, I was President Reagan's domestic policy adviser, and before that, undersecretary of education. I'd given hundreds of interviews. FRC has published a monthly newsletter for years. We put out reams of policy papers. I do a daily radio commentary that goes out over hundreds of stations. I've written two books on public-policy issues. But I knew Rather wasn't looking for policy briefs and issue papers—material his staff had no doubt already examined.

I made my reply personal and intimate. "I want to see an America," I said, "where I don't have to worry about date rape when my daughter goes out for the first time at college. I want an America where, when a young man pledges to love and cherish and honor her for the rest of their lives, there's a good chance he means it. I want a country where children come first again and where virtue is honored; a place where values matter and the American dream is still real. I want a country where families no longer have to hide behind barred windows, where criminals do real time and aren't released on a whim or a technicality. I want a place where children can play in public parks again without fear, and where adults can walk across those parks at night.

"I yearn for a country where women are recognized and praised for their achievements in science, art, and business. But I also yearn for a nation where a woman who would rather be home with her children is no longer subjected to the disdain of the common culture and where the best compliment you can pay someone is that 'He's a good family man.' I want a place where government quits robbing us of the fruits of our labor so that more families can get by on one salary.

"The flickering light that shines from the windows of our nation's houses at night would more often be from the hearth, where 'family fireside chats' are taking place, and less often from the drone of television sets. Families would spend more time being real families, not watching artificial ones.

"I hope for a land where love of country is seen as a virtue again. Where the young are taught the unique blessing they have received just to have been born in such a place.

"In my America, the schools would work once more. Political correctness would be thrown out, and the goal of education would once again be to teach our children to have 'knowing heads and loving hearts.'

"In this land, racism, quotas, and special rights would be rejected, and all our children would be taught to judge their fellow citizens by the content of their character, not the color of their skin. I see a country that respects life again—where drive-by shootings and one and a half million aborted babies each year are seen as a disaster. Here responsibilities would be as important as rights, and a handshake would be something to rely on. In my country, working men and women would be praised, not penalized by ever-growing government. The truly poor would get a hand up, not a handout."

As I went on to describe in detail what had led me to forsake a lucrative law practice or a high-paying corporate lobbying job and instead devote my life to defending traditional values in Washington, I saw Dan Rather's head begin to nod in agreement. Whether or not he had come to interview me with a stereotype in mind, at that moment he seemed to be hearing for the first time who I was and what people like me hope for our country. And in that moment, I decided to write down the vision that became this book.

This is my attempt to reach out to all Americans of goodwill, to introduce myself and the movement of which I'm a part. Two recent polls in the *Washington Post* and *Los Angeles Times* confirm once again that a majority of Americans share many of our convictions.[1] Yet for a lot of you reading this work, this will be your first direct contact with us. You've doubtless heard us described in the media. Let this be our time of getting to know one another without the bright lights and the famous reporters' bylines coming between us. But many of you reading this book already know us and share our concerns. For you, I hope this work will help to reinforce deeply held beliefs and give the encouragement that comes when we see a public defense of the ideals we honor.

✦ 2 ✦

The Best of Times and the Worst of Times

The famous opening line of Charles Dickens's classic novel *A Tale of Two Cities* says, "It was the best of times, it was the worst of times." Even though Dickens wrote those words to describe eighteenth-century England and France, they're also a perfect description of the United States as we approach the twenty-first century. Like most of us, I see many reasons to celebrate America and our accomplishments. But there is also much that's troubling about our future.

We're at peace overseas, but fierce struggles rage within our borders.

We've produced more wealth than any nation in history, but our children all too often seem to lack a sense of purpose or direction.

Our military power is second to none, but we seem more divided about basic issues than at any time since the Civil War.

I don't want to sound like a pessimist, because I'm not. I'd like to emphasize that fact here at the start of this book, because the news media would often have you believe otherwise. So let's look briefly at some of what's good about America.

The United States has accomplished a great deal in this incredible century. Just think about our recent history. We provided the leadership to defeat the two great "isms" of the twentieth century—first nazism and its Japanese allies in World War II, followed by the defeat of Soviet communism in the 1980s.

Born in 1946, I didn't experience the Depression and the war years firsthand. But my parents' lives, and the lives of millions like them, were shaped by those tumultuous events. My father was with the First Marine Division in the bloody South Pacific. He relived agonies telling me what it was like to spend day after day far from home, fighting for his family and the survival of our country. My mother told me what it felt like to wake up on a Sunday morning and hear the news that we had been the victim of a surprise attack at Pearl Harbor. It's hard to imagine the fear and anxiety that gripped people from one end of the country to the other as word spread of the infamous assault. In the months that followed, Americans legitimately worried whether we would lose that war, and also about the implications of having a foreign power conquer our nation.

Though Pearl Harbor was a traumatic event for our country, I read in Winston Churchill's diary that he enjoyed his soundest sleep of the war the night after it occurred. He knew that as horrifying as the news was, the final outcome of the war was now sealed. The democracies would prevail. He had no doubt that once the United States brought to bear its economic might and the bravery of its young men, Hitler's and Japan's legions would be routed. Churchill knew the capabilities of free men and women, of what he called the "American race," better than we ourselves did.

After V-E Day and V-J Day, America was tired, but there was no time to rest. Soon we found ourselves in the great "stare-down" with the Soviet Union that history calls the Cold War. In the years that followed, we had to spend hundreds of billions of dollars of our tax money to buy the weapons systems and build the alliances that would stop communism. We drew a line in Europe and in Asia, and we invested our treasure to make sure the Iron Curtain would never fall over the free world. It was a job that often divided us, and the economic sacrifices it entailed were high.

In the long run, however, the money we spent didn't matter that much. A rich, free nation can replace and rebuild economic assets. But the Cold War required us to do more than open our wallets. To preserve liberty, we once again were required to send our sons to fight and die, this time in places like Porkchop Hill, Da Nang, and many others, the names of which too many of us have already forgotten. These young men, blood of our blood, flesh of our flesh, died for a great cause, even though at times too many in our nation seemed ungrateful.

How about our economic system? Here, too, the record is, on balance, good. True, there have been boom times and bad, recessions and recoveries, periods of decline and of expansion. All economic systems are subject to such fluctuations. But if we examined one long chart that showed how the U.S. economy has progressed from 1900 to today, we would see a gently swelling line of increasing prosperity.

Our system of democratic capitalism has provided more opportunity and jobs than any other system in the world. Our example is being copied by one emerging nation after another as they try to provide opportunity and jobs for millions of their own citizens. Socialism is in retreat. It still has advocates on the faculties of a few American colleges and in a few congressional committees that don't understand the trend toward free enterprise. But advocates of state-controlled economies are losing ground to those who believe people should have the right to earn, save, and invest free of government meddling.

What about American ideals? Our political beliefs are triumphant over much of the world. During the student revolt in China in 1989, for instance, the dissidents marched through the streets of China's capital. They didn't carry the "little red book" of Chairman Mao, or even the wisdom of Confucius. Instead, they waved copies of our Declaration of Independence. They made papier-mâché models of our Statue of Liberty. There's not a tyrant in the world who sleeps easily tonight, because the hopes and dreams of people everywhere have been inspired by the great words of our founding documents.

Bill Bennett, the former secretary of education, has long spoken to students about what he calls "the gates test." "What happens to a country," he asks, "when it opens its gates?" In many countries, the people run out as fast as their feet will carry them. But here in the United States, whether the gates are open or closed, people will do anything to get *in*.

We are now having a long overdue debate about illegal immigration. But as the debate progresses, let's not lose sight of why we have the problem. The reason is that our nation is a beacon of hope to the world. People everywhere still want to come to this country to find a better life for themselves and their children.

THE REAL NATIONAL PRODUCT

All of us could add to the list of good things the United States has accomplished, from our technological advances to medical breakthroughs. But such a list tells only half the story. In spite of all our achievements, most of us instinctively know something has gone wrong in our country.

For nearly a decade now, a majority of Americans of all races and economic levels have told pollsters that they believe our country is headed in the wrong direction. In the past, that finding tracked with our economy. In good times, people were optimistic. Today's poll results, however, suggest Americans aren't thinking about the gross national product (GNP), but rather about the state of our hearts and souls.

As just one example of many I could mention, a poll conducted by Family Research Council in October 1995 showed that 66 percent of Americans believe "things have pretty seriously gotten off on the wrong track," compared with only 21 percent who believe things are on the right track. Moreover, the majority (61 percent) of those who think America is going the wrong way cite "the breakdown of the family and a decline in values" rather than economic problems.[1]

Historians and philosophers have come up with many ways to judge a great nation. It's possible to look at the size of its GNP, the strength and reach of its military, or the gleam of its cities. By those measures and many others, America is a great, great country that has drawn millions of pilgrims across stormy seas.

But it's also possible to measure a nation by the health of its children and the strength of its families, by the safety of its streets and the values of its culture. On any given night in America, too many children cry themselves to sleep. Too many long for the arms of a father who isn't there; too many have been damaged by pornography, drug addiction, or venereal disease; too many have been abused and exploited. Too many families are broken, too many schools aren't educating, and too many homes have bars on their windows. By those measures, the United States is falling far short of our Founders' dreams.

I recently read a story about a public-school teacher in California. She had worked in the Los Angeles schools many years and had a reputation as a good teacher. Then she left the profession to start her own family. She and her husband had several children, raised them well, and eventually sent the last child off to college.

At that point, because of her love for children and learning, she decided to return to the teaching profession. On her first day back on the job, she walked into the classroom and began the way she always had in the past. "Good morning, children," she said, to which her former students had always responded, "Good morning, Mrs. Jones."

But on this day, when she greeted her students, a young thug in the front row shouted back, "Shut up, bitch!" And everybody in the room laughed.

The teacher later asked, "What happened in America between 'Good morning, Mrs. Jones' and 'Shut up, bitch'? And who's going to do something about it?"

Those are fair questions.

WHAT WENT WRONG?

What went wrong with America? First, I believe that as a nation, we have forgotten God. Now, I know that statement will sound foreign to the ears of some modern Americans. But that in and of itself is a symptom of the problem. For most of our 220 years as a nation, America's political leadership and much of our citizenry have been animated by the belief that America has a special role in God's historic plan. Many books have been written on the subject. Lincoln called us the "almost chosen people." He also believed that the Civil War was a form of penance for the national sin of slavery. I don't think there's another nation whose leaders have more consistently summoned the people to meditate on and give thanks for the blessings God has bestowed on them.

I also believe that when a nation violates the natural order of things, it pays a terrible price. For example, the Judeo-Christian tradition—indeed, as C.S. Lewis pointed out in *The Abolition of Man*, nearly *all* ethical and religious traditions—teach that sexual promiscuity is wrong and that sex should be enjoyed only within the marriage covenant. But now American elites reject that view, as do many ordinary citizens, and as a result, modern American life is littered with the broken bodies and abandoned women and children of the sexual revolution.

In each case where we have abandoned the "natural law," we have suffered greatly.

A second and related problem is the separation, in our culture and most of the Western world, of virtue from liberty. The Founders were unanimous in their view that only a virtuous people could remain free. The reason is simple: Virtue restrains our passions and desires. When people do everything the law may allow, they turn their societies into jungles. Our system of limited government and the Constitution itself were designed with the assumption that the people were virtuous.

James Madison, coauthor of the Constitution and our fourth president, told the Virginia Ratifying Convention in 1788, "To suppose that any form of government will secure liberty or happiness without any virtue in the people, is a chimerical idea."[2]

President George Washington underscored this

theme in his farewell address, delivered in September 1796: "'Tis substantially true that virtue or morality is a necessary spring of popular government. . . . Can it be that Providence has not connected the permanent felicity of a Nation with its virtue?"[3]

John Adams, our second president, echoed that sentiment 15 years later, writing, "Religion and virtue are the only foundations, not only of republicanism and of all free government, but of social felicity under all governments and in all the combinations of human society."[4]

Eventually, the unrestrained passions of people cause government to grow larger and more oppressive. We've seen that pattern in our own nation in the last 40 years. When parents don't meet familial responsibilities, a government bureaucrat will always be ready to take over the task. Are people afraid of being robbed or mugged? Some government official will suggest you give up your civil liberties for security or recommend we all need a national identity card to make law enforcement easier. This book contains a lot of good policy ideas about how government can improve our society. But the most important recommendations are aimed at you, the reader, in your role as a parent or child, citizen, voter, employee, or entrepreneur. And the last chapter is a call for all of us to make a compact with each other to govern ourselves better so that America can be restored.

The third thing that has happened is that we've allowed politicians, particularly in Washington, to become our masters instead of our servants. History has shown that when a free people come to rely on government to provide for them, they will eventually become corrupted. It's no accident that the nation with the highest rate of nonmarital births is Sweden, where social welfare spending climbed rapidly in the first half of this century. "Welfare," Franklin Roosevelt said, "is a narcotic, a subtle destroyer of the human spirit."

Our freedom doesn't come from Washington, D.C. Our Declaration of Independence tells us that liberty is a birthright and that while tyrannical governments can temporarily abridge it, it is nonetheless inalienable—that is, it can't be taken away. Liberty's source is God, and the guarantee of it in our country is the first "contract with America," the Constitution.

A SHINING CITY ON A HILL

When President Reagan left office in 1989, he delivered his farewell address on television. It was just days before George Bush was sworn in, and, naturally enough, most Americans were more attentive to the new administration. But I will never forget that January night and the hopeful message Ronald Reagan left with us. He had always seen the United States the way John Winthrop saw it over 350 years ago. She would be "a shining city on a hill," Reagan said. She would be well defended by strong walls, but her walls would have gates through which commerce and travelers could pass in peace and safety.

I like the way President Reagan always referred

to America as "she." It was old-fashioned, true, and sentimental. But his language harkened back to a time when great ships and great states could claim the service, loyalty, and unfeigned love of the people. Ronald Reagan was a successful president, I believe, because he really believed in the ideals he defended, and because he had an uncommon ability to communicate those ideals to the average American.

I know Ronald Reagan, and I share his basic optimism about the American people. When I worked in the White House, I knew I had a fighting chance of carrying a pro-family position on an issue if I could talk to him.

Many of us remember the election of 1980. We recall the television maps of the country turning a bright "Reagan blue" as state after state marched into the Californian's ranks. It was a stunning moment. The people had spoken. Such a moment occurred again in November 1994. The 40-year hold of one party on the U.S. House of Representatives was broken in a sharp and dramatic departure from the past. Congress, statehouses, and hundreds of legislative seats changed hands.

As remarkable as those changes were, I ask you to imagine one even more profound and far-reaching. What if you were to awaken tomorrow morning to find the newspaper headlines reporting "Pro-Family Movement Sweeps the Nation!" Suppose this sweep included not simply political offices, but also the anchor of the evening news, the president of the local college, and your neighborhood school's PTA. In short, suppose we reestablished the cultural consensus that once existed in this country about the importance of family. What would the America look like that I and others want to build? How would it affect your future and your children? Do we have a vision for our country that could make a difference?

I challenge you to dream great dreams. My children have been taught to expect great days ahead for themselves and our country. Forget the naysayers and the "gloom and doom" crowd. Our 220-year history has been marked time and again by victory against all odds.

Who could have predicted that a relatively small colonial outpost could take on the great British Empire and emerge triumphant? But we did. And every step of the way since, we've defied the odds. Hearty and brave, God-fearing and bold, Americans have tamed a great wilderness and brought free government to much of the world.

We can find our way out of our troubles. Events have occurred in our time that are little short of miraculous. We have watched as the Berlin Wall came tumbling down and the red flag was lowered over the Kremlin. Americans can recapture the spirit of enterprise and assert our moral confidence. Failed policies and flawed worldviews need not hold us hostage. This book is a call for better government, but perhaps more important, it's a call for better citizenship. I hope that in it you will find solutions you can embrace to make America "a shining city on a hill" once again.

What follows in these pages is my description of

the absolute minimum we must do to restore an America that honors families and safeguards the young. Each of nine chapters is devoted to a major policy area, from crime, to education, to culture, to the priority of family, to the sanctity of human life. At the beginning of each of these chapters, I tell a true story illustrating the need for change in the area under consideration. Most of these stories, sadly, are taken from my swiftly growing file of recent assaults on the American family. The story is followed by a meditation on what our nation would look like if the goals of the pro-family movement were realized.

Let me mention an aside here. This statement of our goals is important not only for what it includes, but also for what it rules out. In the past year, politicians and columnists have relentlessly scourged pro-family conservatives, charging them with seeking to impose everything from a theocracy to a totalitarian form of government. One glance at the major themes in this book, however, makes it clear that the restoration we seek would come primarily from individual changes of heart and would lead inevitably to *smaller*, less-pervasive government.

Next, each chapter details a half dozen or more public-policy prescriptions, changes we can and should make to put this nation back on the solid foundations of family, faith, and freedom. Each chapter then closes with a list of questions that will help you hold to account the men and women who represent you in elective office. In the end, what will matter for this country is not where I stand but where you stand—and whether you're willing to ask of all who would serve you *where they stand* as well.

Accountability and reliability must be restored to our system of government. The long journey of the U.S. citizen—worker, parent, and patriot—is like the long journey of the figure in Robert Frost's poem. All of us have "promises to keep" and "miles to go" before we sleep. Our political system, we know, may fail the people, but it will never be better than the people. That's why this book concludes with a compact that every citizen can sign as a statement of the mutual obligations we hold to one another. Whatever course our political leadership follows, we the people—we whose ancestors established this form of government and saw it through the crash of economies and the clash of arms—will have signed over to one another, as our Founders did of old, our lives, our fortunes, and our sacred honor. It will take nothing less than this to keep the promise of a pro-family America.

✦ 3 ✦

Americanism for Today

Recently, I met Captain Scott O'Grady. I invited him to our office to give him our Family, Faith, and Freedom Award. He's the young U.S. Air Force flier who bailed out of his stricken jet over Bosnia and successfully evaded capture for six days. His rescue was what Churchill would have called "a miracle of deliverance," and Captain O'Grady was the first to acknowledge it. After humbly thanking the brave marines who had snatched him out of harm's way— "like a scared little rabbit," he modestly said—Captain O'Grady gave the glory to God. Scott O'Grady is an American hero straight out of central casting. He's the kind of hero Hollywood has belatedly recognized our yearning for with a blockbuster movie like *Apollo 13*.

Captain O'Grady is also the sort of young man who amazed General Eisenhower during World War II when he marveled, "Where do we get such men?" The easy answer is, we get them from the same places we've always gotten them: from Tupelo, Mississippi, Columbus, Ohio, and Captain O'Grady's Spokane, Washington. We get them from every region, from farms and cities, villages and towns. What's unusual today is that we don't spend more time honoring these heroes.

My daughter Elyse joined our entire family in watching the television networks' fiftieth anniversary D-day specials in June 1994. She was well-equipped for this special event in her senior year at one of northern Virginia's best public high schools. She had heard the family stories, of course, especially the ones about her paternal grandfather, "Spike," who was a marine in the Pacific during World War II. Our family was thrilled at the fine job the networks did in portraying the uncommon valor that was in fact common for so many young Americans during that fateful Normandy invasion.

We were astonished, however, when Elyse went back to school and more than a few of her fellow students exclaimed, "I've never heard of this before!" My wife, Carol, and I were amazed. How could that be? How could the young people in one of the best public-school systems in our country not know of those unparalleled acts of devotion and courage?

We who live in the Washington area can hardly overlook the many monuments to our country's past. The Iwo Jima monument depicts the intrepid marines who braved fanatical Japanese resistance to raise the Stars and Stripes atop Mount Suribachi. Even our subway stops—DuPont, McPherson, Farragut—recall heroes of the Civil War.

I'm always impressed with the Vietnam Veterans Memorial. Whenever I start to get discouraged or

frustrated, I make it a point to visit that deeply affect-
ing place. I know there was much controversy about
the memorial when it was first conceived and built.
Many fine vets who had put their lives on the line
were offended by the somber black stone, polished to
a mirror finish and engraved with the names of more
than 58,000 young Americans who lost their lives in
Southeast Asia. But I think that controversy has now
passed, washed away by the tears of millions.

I never fail to wonder at the way people from all
over the country come to that memorial to touch the
stone and trace the name of a beloved father, son,
daughter, sister, or brother. The people have changed
that memorial, too. Unled by any official, unguided
by any government regulation, Americans began
leaving mementos at the base of "the Wall" or in its
crevices. Each day now, you can see people lovingly
depositing a rose, a poem, pictures of children whom
the loved and lost never saw, a family Bible, keys to
that favorite Mustang, sometimes even a six-pack of
beer. The tokens are as varied as the people themselves. But each one comes from the heart. And each
night, the dutiful rangers of the National Park Service
collect those offerings for safekeeping. At dawn, the
simple and sincere acts of homage begin anew.

A VISION FOR A BETTER FUTURE

Although few visitors to the Vietnam Veterans
Memorial say it in so many words, their selfless devotion goes beyond the friend or family member who

served in that divisive war. These Americans, unbidden by any official command, come to pay their personal tribute to the idea of America, to the still-strong belief that this favored land has a special place in the unfolding of history. Just as Americans have been greatly blessed, so we also have a great responsibility. And to believe in this sense of America's special mission is not out of fashion among the good and common people of our country. Even if our cultural elites consider it hopelessly naive and unbearably unsophisticated, I'm convinced that every American child should be taught "a decent respect" for the kind of sacrifice represented by the Vietnam Veterans Memorial.

We should do this because we are, in the words of "The Star-Spangled Banner," "a heav'n rescued land." We should teach these patriotic values because we have a higher responsibility than other countries. In this century alone, Americans have repeatedly risked, and laid down, their lives for the freedom of others. This by itself should command respect. But there's another compelling reason as well: our own safety. As C.S. Lewis wrote, "We laugh at honor and are shocked to find traitors in our midst." Can we really be surprised at the John Walker spy ring in the navy or the Aldrich Ames espionage case in the CIA—both involving traitors who sold their country's secrets for money—when we have failed to uphold the virtues of fidelity, valor, and honor?

Patriotism doesn't just happen. During the American Revolution, General Washington issued an order during a critical moment: "Let only Americans stand watch this night." He was actively teaching his freezing, starving men—many of whom thought of themselves as first Hampshiremen, Marylanders, and Virginians—what it meant to be Americans. He was entrusting them with their country's destiny, and they knew it. I believe we must be no less prepared to entrust our country's destiny to my daughter's generation. These youngsters are the future of America, and it's our duty to prepare them for that burden and that glory.

Patriotism means loyalty to our country above all others. In the Oath of Citizenship that naturalized citizens are required to swear, new Americans pledge to "renounce and abjure all allegiance and fidelity to any foreign prince, potentate, state or sovereignty of whom or which I have heretofore been a subject or citizen."

This issue of patriotism is raised whenever Americans are required to put themselves under the authority of the United Nations (UN). A recent case in Germany, involving SPC Michael New, a young U.S. Army medic, shows this. Assigned to Macedonia, New refused to wear the blue beret and shoulder patch of the UN. He had sworn an oath, he said, to defend the Constitution of the United States, not the world body.

Without getting into the legal intricacies of "lawful orders" and U.S. treaty obligations or prejudging SPC New's case, I can say that we undermine the loyalty and patriotism of our all-volunteer forces when we order them to serve under foreign officers and foreign flags. Most of our young men who died in

PROPERTY OF
BROADWAY CHRISTIAN CHURCH LIBRARY
910 BROADWAY
FORT WAYNE, IN 46802

Somalia were serving in U.S. units that had to share vital intelligence with unreliable foreign forces. Few of those other soldiers serving in multinational operations had the courage or determination to rescue our boys from murderous mobs.

During our Revolutionary War, the French general Lafayette commanded American troops, but he did so as an American officer, subject to the orders and discipline of General Washington. Similarly, U.S. troops in World War I fought in the trenches in France, but they were under our General Pershing's orders. Even in Korea, which was a UN "police action," Americans served unambiguously under the American flag and were led by American officers.

We owe it to every young person in our armed forces—and to their families—to give them the best support, the best training, and the best leadership we can. That means we owe them the capable leadership of U.S. officers and the honor and protection of the American flag.

POLICY RECOMMENDATIONS

It's not hard to imagine how the United States could realize its destiny as "this home of freedom."

1. All parents should be able to choose a school for their children where the day begins with the Pledge of Allegiance, our national anthem, and a moment of reverent silent reflection. These ideas are what Lincoln meant when he spoke of "the mystic chords of memory" that stretch from every patriot

BROADWAY CHRISTIAN CHURCH LIBRARY
910 BROADWAY
FORT WAYNE, IN 46802

grave to every American heart. Parents should be able to choose a school where fidelity is a treasured part of the curriculum. They should be offered teachers willing to acknowledge that the United States is not simply another country, but one that has always had a sense of a higher calling. If every college and professional athletic game can start with "The Star-Spangled Banner"—and it's rare that anyone remains seated—there should be no reason why schools cannot impart the same bracing sense of America's special mission.

2. Our schools should offer a thorough study of the Declaration of Independence. Washington ordered it to be read to his troops. Jefferson was so quietly proud of it that he listed it on his tombstone as one of his three greatest accomplishments. Lincoln said he never had a political idea that did not come from it.

If we think it's old hat, we should recall that Dr. Martin Luther King Jr. quoted the Declaration's stirring words from the steps of the Lincoln Memorial on that memorable day in 1963 when he gave his famous "I Have a Dream" speech. Young Chinese students, demonstrating for democracy in Tienanmen Square in 1989, were clutching copies of it when they were gunned down by communist despots.

How better to teach individual worth and self-esteem? We are, each one of us, *created equal*. We are, no matter how poor, how unintelligent, or how unwanted, *endowed by our Creator with certain unalienable rights*.

That's why slavery and abortion have always led

to an "irrepressible conflict." The truth of human
equality and human dignity, which is laid out by the
Declaration and is the justification for the existence of
this country, cannot be reconciled with either of those
practices. Slavery and abortion are an affront to the
very philosophy upon which the United States of
America is based.

When Jefferson wrote that "we hold these truths
to be self-evident," he didn't mean no one could dispute them. Many people did dispute them in his time.
Many more have disputed them since. What Jefferson
and the other signers of the Declaration of Independence meant was that "these truths" were being put
forward as the foundation upon which the whole
argument for independence would be based. It was,
to the mathematically minded Jefferson, just like
advancing an axiom as the basis for a proof in geom-
etry. That's why it's vital our children be taught the
philosophy of the Declaration in detail.

3. **Every American parent should be able to
choose a school where mastery of the English language is the first order of business**. Federal bilingual
education laws have been a disaster. As a friend who
served in the Reagan administration with me once
remarked, bilingual education threatens to make millions of kids illiterate in *two* languages. You cannot
appreciate our country's heritage of freedom unless
you can read the English language. We're denying
millions of young Americans the chance to participate
in the larger life of our country when we fail to insist
that they be taught English first.

English first doesn't mean English only. I come from the Midwest, and I'm well aware that millions of loyal and patriotic Americans spoke German in the home well into the 1940s. We've always had immigrant families where grandmothers and grandfathers looked to the younger generation to translate for them. We've also had a lively foreign language press. Today the biggest controversy is over Spanish. Tomorrow, it could be Haitian French or Hong Kong Chinese. We need to make it clear that English is the gateway to democracy and commerce in America. We will likely find that foreign-language speakers will themselves appreciate and approve our efforts in behalf of their children. That's why, when Californians voted on English as an official language in 1994, the measure carried even heavily Hispanic precincts.

4. A country where children daily salute the flag is unlikely to be one where that flag is spitefully burned. A constitutional amendment to put an end to such outrageous displays is long overdue. I've never seen an issue that so sharply divided the lawyers from the people. As a lawyer myself, I can appreciate the concern many in my profession claim for our civil liberties. But I can assure you there are no monuments in Washington to the lawyers who have sacrificed their lives for their country and the freedom of their fellow citizens. This is the flag that graces the caskets of our fallen heroes. This is the only flag that's displayed on the moon. Americans *want* to honor it. The court rulings that say laws against desecration are unconstitutional are a prime example of the tyranny of the unelected.

A PATRIOTIC PEOPLE

Not everything necessary for restoring patriotism can or should be done by government. When G.K. Chesterton, the British writer, visited the United States early in this century, he was amazed at the unity and patriotism we displayed. "America is a country with the soul of a church," he wrote. He didn't mean we all worshiped the same way. We didn't then. We didn't when Washington let his soldiers choose their own chaplains. We certainly don't subscribe to one religious belief today. But Chesterton meant we had a reverence for our country that was like that which many religious people have for their faith. Some intellectuals have criticized this intense passion for America. Marxist professors have even expressed their frustration with what they call "American exceptionalism." Yet few can deny we are an extraordinarily patriotic people.

Our schools should naturally be the places where that patriotism is deepened and strengthened. We must do everything we can to bring that about. But there are also many things we can do as families before this important task is accomplished in our nation's classrooms.

Contact one of your local veterans' organizations. Ask how you can participate in their ceremonies at a national cemetery or town war memorial. Young children are particularly welcome to place wreaths and carry small American flags at Veterans Day and Memorial Day observances. If your local Scout troops don't sell red poppies to support veterans' groups anymore, urge them to take up the tradition once again.

Veterans' hospitals can often use volunteers. Teens can benefit from the one-on-one contact with those aging vets who have given so much to each of us.

Make an oral history of your family's experience of World War II. Go through those old trunks in the attic; search out and make copies of the fading photographs. Check out some of the old issues of *Life, Look,* and, especially, the *Saturday Evening Post* on microfilm. Your local librarian can help.

Plan a "Canteen Night" at your church, synagogue, or neighborhood center. Get tapes of the wartime hits of Glenn Miller, Benny Goodman, the Andrews Sisters, and the Mills Brothers. Rent some classic videos, like Frank Capra's *Why We Fight* and the English favorite *Mrs. Miniver.* Ask a veteran to describe his or her experiences during the war. Finish the evening by joining in the singing of Irving Berlin's moving song "God Bless America." Or offer your youth group a Saturday series of movies like *The Longest Day, Tora, Tora, Tora,* and the highly acclaimed documentary *World at War.* Allow time for adults to discuss the films with the youngsters.

✦ ✦ ✦

Questions for Those Who Would Lead Us

When we, the people, choose our leaders through the democratic process, we should not be impressed by the Pepsodent smile, the well-coifed hairdo, or the slick promises. We have the right and the duty to ask probing questions. We should always be civil. But civility, as Jack Kennedy said, is not a sign of weakness. When we get the chance, let's ask the candidates who would serve us what they would do to restore patriotism in our country.

Here are some sample questions:

1. How will you restore respect for our country and its history?
2. What will you do to reestablish the highest standards of loyalty and character for security clearances?
3. What practical measures will you take to assure that all parents may choose schools where America's heroes are honored and where voluntary prayer is permitted?
4. What will you do to make sure that young people learn English in our schools?
5. What will you do about public displays of contempt for the flag?
6. How will you safeguard America's national sovereignty?
7. What will you do to assure that America's young fighting men and women serve only under American commanders and obey lawful orders given only by American military and civilian leaders?

◆ 4 ◆

Feeling Safe in Our Streets

It's every urban family's nightmare—making a wrong turn onto one of the "mean streets" of our big cities. The nightmare became reality in the summer of 1995 when a family inadvertently drove down the "Avenida Assecinos," the street of killers, in the Cypress Gardens section of Los Angeles. Within seconds, gang members formed a gauntlet, throwing trash cans in front of the family's car to block its way while gunfire rang out. By the time the incident was over, three-year-old Stephanie Kuhen was fatally shot, her two-year-old brother was wounded in the foot, and the driver was shot in the back.

"It was just the wrong place, the wrong time," one L.A. police detective said. "It could happen to anybody." And in fact it does happen all the time, not only to "strangers," but also to the struggling families who have to live and work in the neighborhoods like the one where Stephanie died. Residents in that part of Cypress Gardens say they hear gunshots several times each week, and many don't let their children play outside for fear of stray bullets.[1]

No American should have to live that way. No family should be one wrong turn away from murder.

A generation or so ago, my grandparents slept with their doors unlocked—this in the middle of the crushing poverty of the Great Depression. Today, locks are everywhere, and law-abiding citizens find them-selves with iron bars on their windows when it's the criminals who should be behind bars.

The personal security business is booming. Ninety percent of Americans agree that crime is a "serious" problem and getting worse.[2] Eighteen percent of us have burglar alarms in our homes, and half of Ameri-can households have guns for protection.[3] Americans have also hired 1.5 million private police officers in the belief that public law enforcement is unable to deal with the tidal wave of violence.[4] Our government is failing in its primary task of protecting its citizens from harm.

Most Americans know our criminal justice system is on the wrong road. Every day, more of us are seized with fear and don't know what to do. Sadly, unless we make some basic changes, there's little reason to expect a better future.

In fact, experts project that within the next decade, the United States will experience an unprecedented surge in youth crime.[5] A future crop of teenage "bar-barians," already born to families devoid of love, discipline, and supervision, bathed in the glare of ceaseless, gratuitous media violence, are living in communities marked by random and mindless crime. What's America to do?

Millions of Americans have abandoned the cities

and sought safe haven in the suburbs; but are they any safer? The fact is, there is no escape—at least 10 million citizens will be victims of violent crime this year, and 32 million will be victims of property crime.[6] Drive-by shootings and the drug trade, once confined to our big cities, are now plaguing small and midsized communities all over the country.

According to U.S. Justice Department statistics, there is one violent crime every 16 seconds; one murder every 21 minutes; one forcible rape every five minutes; one robbery every 48 seconds; one aggravated assault every 28 seconds; and one property crime every three seconds.[7]

The American Medical Association (AMA) has given the country a failing grade on public violence. Robert E. McAfee, the AMA's president, in announcing its 1995 "National Report Card on Violence," labeled violence the number-one public health issue. McAfee said, "The tide of violent behavior does not show any signs—any signs—of turning."[8]

Besides the personal tragedy of millions of crimes, the direct and indirect economic cost to Americans is between $425 billion and $674 billion annually.[9] That includes $128 billion—an amount equivalent to 69 percent of all after-tax corporate profits—in direct business losses, litigation expenses, and security outlays.[10]

The truth is that law enforcement is overwhelmed. In the 1960s, the United States had 3.3 police officers for every violent crime reported.[11] In 1993, the reverse was true, with 3.47 violent crimes reported for every police officer.

The crime clearance rate (number of crimes solved as a percentage of crimes reported) is another good indicator of the problem. In 1965, the national homicide clearance rate was 91 percent. But in the past two years, that rate stood at only 65.5 percent.[12] With the homicide rate rising and the clearance rate plummeting, more murderers escape the criminal justice system's reach. Frighteningly, the annual murder rate is projected to rise from 24,526 in 1993 to possibly 40,000 a year in the next decade.[13]

A VISION FOR A BETTER FUTURE

The United States can and must do better than this. In the country the pro-family movement hopes to build, our families could walk, play, and work on city streets again without fear. Parks and bicycle trails would belong to law-abiding citizens day and night—not to thugs. Our children could go to school and not fear gunfire in the halls or on the playground. They could learn without harassment from drug pushers.

Victims of crimes would get as much attention and consideration from our courts and legal system as we currently shower on criminals. And lawbreakers would pay restitution to those who have suffered financial or other losses at their hands.

There would be truth in sentencing—not to mention safety for the public—a 20-year sentence would actually mean 20 years in jail instead of two years and easy parole. Repeat felons would be kept behind bars.

In an America serious about crime, personal responsibility would be the standard again. No longer would psychological gibberish, a "bad" upbringing, poverty, or other extraneous conditions serve as an excuse for criminal behavior.

Furthermore, prison time for hard offenses would be "hard time." Prisoners wouldn't live and eat better or have more recreational time than the victims they've exploited.

We want a country where government recognizes safety and security as its number-one reason for existing. We want reform of the juvenile justice system; those who commit adult crimes should be treated and tried as adults. We envision term limits in place for all judges, and impeachment for those who constantly allow thugs back on the street to prey on honest citizens. We want a new ethical code for lawyers that reminds them they are officers of the court who have a stake, with the rest of us, in justice.

We believe that an America back on the right track will also recognize that some crimes are so heinous that those who commit them deserve to pay the ultimate penalty of forfeiting their own lives. We want legal reform that respects our constitutional guarantees but also cuts into the red tape and delays from apparently endless appeals.

POLICY RECOMMENDATIONS

Here are 16 steps that need to be taken now if our dream of a safer America is to be realized:

SENTENCING AND PRISON REFORM

1. Serious repeat violent felons must be put away permanently. Recidivism figures show clearly that many criminals, once released, return to a life of crime.[14] A three-strikes law is badly needed in every state.

In California, the three-strikes law finally passed only after public anger reached the boiling point over the Polly Klaas case. Polly, a 12-year-old, was abducted from her home during a sleep-over with friends and subsequently murdered. Richard Allen Davis, a three-time felon, was charged with the kidnapping and murder. Davis had been released just three months earlier after serving only half a prison sentence for kidnapping.

California's secretary of state, Bill Jones, says the 1994 three-strikes law has cut crime substantially.[15] Los Angeles County Sheriff Sherman Block believes the law is partly responsible for the fact that 6,233 fewer major crimes were committed in the first half of 1994 than during the same period in 1993. The law has also effectively restricted plea bargaining by a number of chronic criminal recidivists.

2. Government must protect the public by keeping violent criminals behind bars for their entire sentences and eliminating bail for violent suspects. Basketball star Michael Jordan can give grim testimony to the value of criminals completing their sentences.

Michael's father, James, was murdered as he sat in his car along Interstate 95. The two teenagers charged with the crime had violent histories. One was on parole after having served only two years of a six-year sentence for attacking a man with an ax. The other was awaiting trial for bashing a convenience store clerk in the head with a cinder block during a robbery. Had these young men been in jail, Mr. Jordan would likely have lived to see Michael return to the basketball court.

3. Adolescents who commit "adult" crimes should be tried as adults and subjected to adult penalties. In Philadelphia, a 16-year-old boy was charged with murdering an ice-cream-truck driver. According to witnesses, the boy stood over the dying man, laughing and making up songs to taunt his victim. Our juvenile justice system was intended to save children from the influence of adult criminals, not to protect them from the consequences of horrific criminal acts. "Children" like that 16-year-old are already lost, and government must make sure our family members do not come face-to-face with such an individual.

4. Criminals must be punished, not pampered. It can be shown that recidivism is high among violent offenders partly because the price they pay for crime is too low. Forty percent of released murderers are rearrested for a felony within three years, and 80 percent of state prison inmates have one or more past convictions.[16]

Consider burglary, for example. Only 7 percent of all burglaries result in an arrest. Of those arrests, only 87 percent are prosecuted and 79 percent convicted. Of those convicted, only 25 percent go to prison. The result is a mere 1.2 percent probability of going to prison for committing burglary, with the average "price" (length of incarceration) being just 4.8 *days*. For rape, the price is 60 days, and for murder, the ultimate crime, only 1.8 years.[17] Clearly, the adage "Crime does not pay" is not applicable to today's judicial system.

5. Other means of punishment, such as restitution, might be used for less-serious offenses. This could help relieve an overburdened prison system. Police are arresting only 44 people for every 100 violent crimes,[18] and the criminal justice system jails only three persons of those arrested.[19] Right now, prison capacity is not the problem. Arresting, convicting, and appropriate sentencing are the challenges. If and when the system begins to be more effective at incarcerating violent offenders, capacity could become a problem.

Victim restitution, either as a substitute for incarceration for less-serious crimes or as a companion to it, should be carefully expanded, even if many inmates are virtually unemployable. For example, a metal factory in Lockhart, Texas, employs 138 inmates at regular wages. The prisoners make computer circuit boards, eyeglasses, and air conditioners. There's a long waiting list to get the few jobs. Prisoners must agree beforehand to give most of their wages to cover the cost of incarceration and/or to aid a victims' compensation fund. Politicians have long passed laws to limit prison-based competition. As a result, prison industries nationwide employ only 9 percent of inmates.[20] This should be changed.

6. No one advocates cruelty or harsh, meaning-less labor such as the old "making little rocks out of big ones," but prisons should be places of punishment, not weight-lifting and entertainment centers. Convicted felons shouldn't be living an easier life than working Americans. Alabama and a few other states have reinstituted chain gangs cleaning up along rural roads. Such "hard time" is appropriate. It also reminds young people of the consequences of breaking the law.

REFORMS IN CRIMINAL PROCEDURE

7. The death penalty, affirmed by the Supreme Court in 1976, must be used if it is to deter crime. The vast majority (80 percent) of Americans support the death penalty,[21] but it is seldom carried out even though, since 1976, more than 5,000 people have received death sentences. Two thousand of those were set aside, but of the remainder, fewer than 300 have been executed. Some convicted killers have lingered on death row nearly 20 years.[22] Used appropriately and carried out swiftly, the death sentence will send a strong signal that some crimes have the most serious consequence to the perpetrator.

8. Habeas corpus loopholes that permit criminals to exploit the courts must be closed. Take, for example, the case of David Ronald Chandler, convicted of ordering the murder of a police informant and sentenced to death. For four years, his lawyers pursued every avenue of appeal. In June 1994, the Supreme Court refused to hear his case. But a week before his scheduled execution, a district-court judge delayed the execution indefinitely to consider new evidence. It's likely that this case will linger in the courts for years and cost taxpayers millions of dollars.

Federal and state habeas corpus reform is necessary to limit the time to appeal a death sentence. It should make frivolous appeals more difficult and, where possible, require prisoners to pay some of the cost for appeals. It should limit stays of execution and mandate the death penalty when aggravating factors outweigh mitigating factors.

9. The exclusionary rule should be changed. Too often, criminals escape prison when critical evidence is excluded from trial because of the way it was obtained. Incriminating evidence found at a crime scene should not be disallowed just because police couldn't get a search warrant in time.

At the same time, Americans are justifiably suspicious of some law enforcement agencies. Tales of police corruption, rogue cops, evidence "planting," and unwarranted or hasty rules of engagement chill our trust. We must have accountable law enforcement in order to allow the criminal justice system to spend less time litigating police misconduct and more time resolving the guilt of defendants.

The watchword in deterring corruption is the same as in deterring any form of criminality: prevention. Corruption occurs when opportunity meets a weakened will. Law enforcement can preclude this meeting by more job rotation. Officers who have been on the same beat for many years sometimes become too familiar with people in their communities whose actions they monitor. The FBI precludes such situations by rotating agents. In addition, better internal controls should be set up to check randomly for abuses. Spot checks by independent investigators who report only to senior officials can expose problems before they mushroom.

10. Jury reform is long overdue. Faced with the often-difficult task of deciding a defendant's fate, jury members ought to be able to ask questions that trial attorneys and prosecutors may miss. They should also be informed of the defendant's past criminal history, especially during sentencing considerations where either mitigating circumstances or a track record of incorrigible behavior is significant.

MORE AGGRESSIVE ENFORCEMENT

11. Increase the prison population to reduce crime. Statistics show that most crime is committed by a core of chronic criminals. Keeping these criminals in jail for longer periods will make society safer, as shown by the experience of California and Texas.

Between 1980 and 1991, the California prison population increased by 314 percent, and serious crime *dropped* 13 percent. During the same period, Texas increased its inmate population by only 73 percent, and serious crime *rose* 28 percent. Those states with the smallest increases in incarceration rates actually averaged almost a 7 percent increase in crime.[23]

Some argue that it costs more to keep a criminal in prison than it would to send him or her to a fine college. The truth, however, is that incarceration is a cost-effective solution to crime as well. The average annual cost to maintain a prisoner is about $25,000, but according to a Rand Corporation survey of 2,190 professional criminals, each criminal committed 187 to 287 crimes a year. With each crime costing society $2,300 on average, the net result is a cost to society of at least $405,000 more than the cost of imprisonment.[24]

12. More local police are necessary to free our citizens to go about their daily lives without fear—to guard our schools, neighborhoods, and commerce. High-visibility police forces can reduce serious crime and maintain order. Cracking down on even minor offenses like vagrancy and traffic violations would signal to society at large a broad elevation of behavioral standards. When police attack public disorder at low levels, they head off trouble of a more serious nature.

13. Government must protect law-abiding citizens from recidivist sex felons. Consider the case of a 30-year-old Columbia, Maryland, mother who was badly beaten and sexually assaulted by a convicted rapist. Thurman Moore, 48, pleaded guilty to the offense but claimed he was not criminally responsible because of mental illness. Incredibly, Moore, convicted three times previously for sexual assault, had just been released early from state prison after serving time for the rape of an 11-year-old schoolgirl.

Enhancing Self-Defense

14. Government should allow and even encourage law-abiding citizens to defend themselves. Unless Americans are encouraged to defend themselves and their property, as Korean-Americans did in Los Angeles during the riots of 1992, they may become enslaved to the dangers of the times.

Criminals choose the time and place for their deeds and rarely do so in the presence of a police officer, so the public must be allowed to defend itself from preying felons. Failing this, violence will continue to flourish, and locked doors will not deter it.

15. Since there are practical limits to how many police can be put into uniform, the constitutionally protected right of law-abiding citizens to keep and bear arms, a proven deterrent to crime, should not be restricted. Professor Joyce Malcolm, writing for the American Bar Foundation in *To Keep and Bear Arms: The Origins of an Anglo-American Right*, had this to say about a citizen's right to bear arms: "The Second Amendment was meant to accomplish two distinct goals. . . . First, it was meant to guarantee the individual's right to have arms for self-defense and self-preservation. . . . These privately owned arms were meant to serve a larger purpose [military service] as well . . . and it is the coupling of these two objectives that has caused the most confusion."[25]

Private gun ownership is constitutionally guaranteed and often necessary today given the increase in criminal violence and the decline in police effectiveness. But just as owning a car or a boat introduces risks and requires responsible use by the owner/operator, so also a gun in the home demands that parents weigh the risks, be properly trained, and take action to keep firearms safely away from children.

Government should adopt both increased penalties for criminals who use guns to commit crimes and the National Rifle Association's recommended national computer registry that would allow instant checks for felony convictions of anyone attempting to buy a firearm.

16. Drugs are the raw explosive for many criminal acts; more can and should be done to reverse the new surge in drug abuse. More than three-fourths of all prison inmates report some history of illicit drug use, and nearly one-third were actually using an illegal drug at the time of their current offense.[26]

Drug abuse also inflicts serious harm on children. Research shows that children who use illicit drugs are significantly more likely to carry a gun to school, take part in gang activities, think of suicide, threaten to hurt others, and get in trouble with the law than children who abstain.[27]

Unfortunately, drug abuse among teenagers has risen greatly in recent years.[28] This surge is attributable to changes in youths' attitudes about the threat associated with illicit drugs.[29] The attitudinal shift can be blamed in part on a popular culture that is increasingly pro-drugs, a lack of consistent national leadership that lovingly guides children to "just say no" to drugs, and declining involvement by parents in the lives of their children.

✦ ✦ ✦

The fact is, government can do only so much, but what it can do, it must do. At the same time, each citizen must be free to defend his or her family and property. Most important, children must be raised to be productive, law-abiding citizens. This is accomplished best in a stable, two-parent family undergirded by traditional values.

Sadly, in the United States today, there's a flight from family responsibility, and the traditional family is increasingly in shambles. Divorce ends half of all American marriages, and the national illegitimacy rate is skyrocketing. Children raised by single, over-extended, and frequently impoverished mothers are at a decided disadvantage. They are far more likely to get into trouble, to become criminals, and to become single mothers while still in their teens. Three-quarters of them will endure a period of poverty before age 18.[30]

For the sake of the children, families must stay together, and they must teach their kids to respect authority. As President James Madison once said, "If men were angels, no government would be necessary." Since men and women aren't angels, however, government must fight crime for what it is—a violent form of selfishness.

✦ ✦ ✦

Questions for Those Who Would Lead Us

1. Will you support laws (three-strikes-and-out, parole reform, etc.) to assure that dangerous and violent felons are imprisoned and serve out their sentences?
2. Will you support the right of all law-abiding Americans "to keep and bear arms" in defense of their lives and property?

3. Will you support restitution—repayment, with penalties, by perpetrators of nonviolent crimes to their victims—in place of jail time?
4. Will you work to allow prosecutors to give juries more background on past offenses by convicted defendants and to present to juries information on the impact of violent crimes on the victims?
5. Will you work for the selection of judges at all levels who will deal severely with those convicted of heinous crimes?
6. Will you lead efforts to restore the forceful and consistent antidrug message that produced so much progress in the drug wars of the 1980s?

◆ 5 ◆

The Worth of a Human Life

On three occasions, I've witnessed the incredible event of the birth of a child. Each time, I found it to be unbelievably exhilarating. The delivery room was filled with shouts of joy from me, Carol, and the attending staffs.

In stark contrast, in September 1995, a courtroom in Queens, New York, was hushed. José Callejas, a father of four, sat on a bench, sobbing quietly. He was anxious, like an expectant dad. He wasn't awaiting the birth of his fifth child, however. He was attending the sentencing of the abortionist responsible for the death of that child and his (José's) wife, Guadalupe Negron. Twenty weeks pregnant, Guadalupe had bled to death from a botched abortion at what the prosecutor called a "filthy, degrading facility"—a perfectly legal facility.

The judge was about to pass sentence. The abortionist, Dr. David Benjamin, made a statement to the court. His speech turned long and rambling, and at one point he referred to the aborted child as a "product of conception."

Judge Robert Hanophy interrupted. "The people in the audience are not familiar with the medical term," he said. "The 'product of conception' is something we used to call a baby."[1]

"We used to call . . ." In a handful of words, Judge Hanophy captured the essence not only of the abortion debate, but also of the debates over euthanasia, assisted suicide, and other sanctity-of-life issues. As these debates have unfolded in modern America, we've changed the words to mask the truth. But we haven't changed—we can't change—the reality. Human life is human life; it is God's, not ours, to take.

That reality is relentless. And, indeed, most Americans recognize that human life begins at conception and that it's wrong to destroy that life. The Supreme Court's abortion decision of 1973 dwelled on viability—that point at which the unborn child is capable of living on its own outside the womb. But only one in five Americans place the beginning of human life that late in pregnancy. According to the survey "Abortion and Moral Beliefs" undertaken by the Gallup Organization in 1991, nearly 56 percent of Americans locate the start of "personhood" at conception, and nearly three-fourths believe it occurs by the time the mother feels the child move in her womb. The same poll found that strong majorities of Americans believe suicide is wrong, even when the person is depressed and lacks "the will to live."[2]

Considering the circumstances under which most Americans would prohibit a particular abortion, and comparing those circumstances with those under which most of the 1.5 million annual U.S. abortions are performed, a 1989 *Boston Globe* survey noted, "Most Americans would ban the vast majority of abortions performed in this country."[3] Conversely, a 1994 survey conducted by Roper-Starch for Focus on the Family found that only 6 percent of Americans want abortion to be available on demand without any restrictions and with government funding of the procedure for poor women.[4] Many Americans may be willing to turn a blind eye to what our incredibly permissive laws allow, but confronted with the reality of abortion, they seek and will support alternatives.

Perhaps all of this is simply the result of intuition about what the violence of abortion implies for the spread of other forms of violence against human beings. Abortion techniques may change, but the truth of what abortion does to blood and brain cannot be suppressed. Likewise, the instrument of euthanasia may be in the hand of a doctor, a family member, or even the patient, but its object is always a human being who feels emotionally or physically abandoned by the human community. And when a baby girl is placed in the darkened corner of a hospital ward and the chart on her crib is marked "No nutrition," she has not been left to die on a windswept hillside, but what's happening to her is still plain and simple infanticide.

Americans of goodwill, conservative or liberal, can ignore such realities only so long. As Christopher Hitchens wrote in the left-wing magazine *The Nation* in 1989:

Anyone who has ever seen a sonogram or has spent even an hour with a textbook on embryology knows that emotions are not the deciding factor. In order to terminate a pregnancy, you have to still a heartbeat, switch off a developing brain and, whatever the method, break some bones and rupture some organs.[5]

George McKenna, writing in the *Atlantic Monthly*, another magazine that has published little in objection to the permissive abortion culture, quoted Hitchens, then said, "Some Americans may succeed in desensitizing themselves to what is going on, as many did with slavery, but most Americans feel decidedly uncomfortable about the stilled heartbeats and brains of 1.5 million human fetuses every year."[6]

McKenna's thesis is that the analogies between slavery and abortion are so strong that they've already been acknowledged by pro-choice leaders, who then have failed to accept the logic of what citizens must do to counter a practice that is legal yet remains utterly "evil." He wrote:

The same formula—grudgingly tolerate, restrict, discourage—that I have applied to abortion is what liberal Democrats have been using to combat racism over the past generation. With abortion, as with racism, we are targeting a practice that is recognized as "wrong" (Hillary Clinton) and "a bad thing" (Kate Michelman). With abortion, as with racism, we are conceding the practical impossibility of outlawing the evil thing itself but pledging the government's best efforts to make it "rare" (Bill Clinton, *et al.*).[7]

A VISION FOR A BETTER FUTURE

What is the pro-family vision of a world where the sanctity of human life is respected? It would be a world in which compassion and a strong moral code stand shoulder to shoulder. Out-of-wedlock pregnancy would be discouraged, but not at the expense of more abortions. All our sons would be taught to temper their sexuality, not to believe that deploying condoms is the mark of consideration toward a date. All our daughters would be taught to believe that saying no isn't just an option but a sign of maturity and the proper prelude to the yes that marriage means.

Crisis pregnancy centers, many of which are already church-affiliated, would be as common and visible in our communities as steeples. It's utopian to believe that no unmarried woman would ever again become pregnant, but those who do would be greeted by a society that has made the avenue of adoption as attractive as it can possibly be. Physicians would once again adhere to the first principle, "Do no harm," and all would take, as the seal of their fidelity to the highest ethics, the restatement of the Hippocratic oath developed by the distinguished physician Joseph Stanton.

For centuries, the Hippocratic oath acted as a powerful constraint on physicians, whatever the law might say for or against a practice they contemplated. Dr. Stanton's restatement has been signed by dozens of prominent physicians. It reads in part:

> I will follow that method of treatment which, according to my ability and judgment, I consider for the benefit of my patient and abstain from all that is harmful or mischievous. I will neither prescribe nor administer a lethal dose of medicine to any patient, even if asked, nor counsel any such thing nor perform act or omission with direct intent deliberately to end a human life. I will maintain the utmost respect for every human life from fertilization to natural death and reject abortion that deliberately takes a unique human life.[8]

Gradually but definitely, the harm that rampant single parenthood has inflicted on our society would be reversed. A mature society can cope with modest numbers of its citizens who have no will to work, who drink excessively or use drugs, or who conceive children without benefit of a wedding band. But we're quickly learning that no society can long endure when majorities behave this way. Such a country will collapse, and the United States can be no exception. The rampant violence in our cities, perpetrated largely by young men who have caught our modern disease of dog-eat-dog individualism, is the fruit of the same relativism that attempts to justify abortion on demand. Abandoning the sanctity-of-life ethic has not delivered us from the clutches of such thugs; it has produced them. They have turned city streets into shooting galleries.

At the same time, the elderly would be respected and cared for, not made to feel as though they're a burden on family or society and, thus, somehow "obligated" to die. Instead, they would be recognized once again as one of our greatest sources of wisdom and love.

POLICY RECOMMENDATIONS

What policies would a pro-family America implement to undergird the sanctity of human life?

1. The conglomerate of taxpayer-financed abortion providers must be disassembled. If the taking of innocent human life is the moral equivalent of slavery, tax exemptions for not-for-profit abortion clinics are as objectionable as they are for racially segregated institutions. Organizations that receive tax money and promote abortion here at home or overseas, such as Planned Parenthood, would be defunded. Government-financed abortions would stop except when the life of the mother is truly in jeopardy.

2. Adoption and foster-care reform must become national priorities. Financial incentives, including substantial tax relief such as the $5,000 adoption credit in the Republican Contract with America, must be passed to promote adoption of infants and older children now caught in the foster-care system. Policies that inhibit adoption, such as curbs on interracial adoption and arbitrary age and income limits, should be dropped. The preferred adoptive family is a married couple that would provide both a mother and a father, but the guiding criterion should be the ability of adoptive parents to love and provide a home, not their race, age, or the splendor of their surroundings. America's children need *value-rich* parents.

3. We should adopt proposals that reform our health-care system to preserve family resources and resist government rationing. Medical savings accounts, tax-preferred benefit plans, and other alternatives to national health insurance must be explored and expanded. Each of these options will strengthen the ability of families to avoid the kind of "managed care" disasters that have characterized nationalized health care in Great Britain and Canada. In the latter, for example, the average waiting period to see an orthopedic specialist is almost 21 weeks.[9] In Britain, almost half of that nation's kidney dialysis centers have refused to treat patients over 65 years of age.[10] No family should be forced to face the choice of bankruptcy or "pulling the plug" on a loved one.

4. The spirit of genuine voluntarism should be renewed. Our nation's network of maternity homes, hospitals, and other voluntary institutions was built primarily on religious commitment. The cost of services was kept down and the personalization of care was maintained because the men and women who entered religious work or medicine were motivated by a spirit of charity. Today voluntarism is often federally subsidized and temporary. We cannot rebuild the institutions that honor the sanctity of life without a resurgence of *lifelong* commitments to voluntary service. In our America, every child would be encouraged to give a year between high school and college to serve his or her country. There are children to be tutored, pains to be eased, and homes to be built!

5. **Experiments on human embryos must be conducted under the same ethical guidelines as research on other human subjects unable to give consent.** Congress, the states, and the private biomedical research community alike should implement policies that reject unethical research on developing human beings. The key principles are that any research contemplated must be designed primarily to benefit the individual undergoing the research, and such research must involve minimal risk of inflicting harm on that individual. Congress must begin this effort by barring all use of federal funds for nontherapeutic experimentation on unborn children. The false science of eugenics—breeding better people or "weeding out the unfit"—should be rejected forever. Such "science" thrives under totalitarianism, but it has no place in a country that believes in the dignity of every human being, including the handicapped.

6. **As the range of life-affirming services to women increases, Congress and the states should implement policies to restrain abortionists by the force of criminal and civil law.** Ronald Reagan, in one of his final pro-life acts as president, issued a proclamation on January 22, 1988, declaring the unalienable personhood of the unborn. His words

made clear that our Constitution, properly understood, already protects the child in the womb. This
was no radical new understanding of the words and
intent of our Founders or of the framers of the Thir-
teenth and Fourteenth Amendments dealing with
slavery; indeed, for more than a century and a half
before the 1973 abortion decision, *Roe v Wade*, our
courts allowed the states to define and increase pro-
tections for the unborn child without interference.

The interference since *Roe* should cease. The states
should have the power to protect the child in the
womb, to protect minors by requiring that parents be
notified when their daughter experiences a pregnancy
or their son causes one, and to protect a husband's
right to know about an impending abortion. At the
same time, Congress should move to limit abortions
and protect the life of the mother by every feasible
means. A "human life bill" can accomplish this goal,
but if the courts once again intervene, an amendment
to the Constitution should be swiftly adopted.

Safeguarding the right to life is not some new idea
that just intruded itself on the American scene. It's one
of those truths, enshrined in the Declaration of
Independence, that we used to call *self-evident*.

✦ ✦ ✦

Questions for Those Who Would Lead Us

1. Will you work to defund Planned Parenthood and
   all other organizations that engage in abortion and
   pro-abortion lobbying?
2. Will you work for reform of our tax laws to

encourage adoption by qualified parents, regardless of race?

3. Will you support medical savings accounts, preferred benefit plans, and other alternatives to medical rationing for the elderly and infirm?

4. Will you require all experiments on embryonic human beings to be conducted only for the benefit of the individual lives involved?

5. Will you oppose public funding of abortion except where the life of the mother would be endangered if the baby were carried to term?

6. Will you support legislation—including, if necessary, a constitutional amendment—that affirms the right to life of every innocent human being, from conception to natural death?

7. Will you take steps to assure the expanded availability of loving alternatives for women faced with a crisis pregnancy?

✦ 6 ✦

The Priority
of Family

The schoolgirls were excited. Tomorrow, they wouldn't have to get up early to go to class. They wouldn't have to turn in any homework, eat any cafeteria food, or worry about being chased by the boys at recess. Tomorrow, they wouldn't have to worry about boys at all. For tomorrow, they would be dressing for success, accompanying their mothers to the office for the 1994 "Take Your Daughter to Work Day." And all the girls were thrilled. All, that is, except Laura Sorrell.

Laura's mom, you see, doesn't work for pay. And while Laura had never before had reason to be embarrassed about her mom's decision to be a mother at home, the officials at Laura's elementary school in Norwood, Ohio, determined that Laura could not spend "Take Your Daughter to Work Day" at home with her mom, learning about homemaking, because they didn't think Laura's mom had a job—at least not a "real" job.

So Laura felt left out. And Laura's mother, Patty Sorrell, felt humiliated by the very school system that often says parents are their children's first and most important teachers.

In response to negative publicity surrounding the incident, the school officials in Norwood eventually reversed their policy. They now permit children interested in celebrating the day with their mothers at home to do so. But the fact that it took a wave of negative publicity for the school administrators in a small, midwestern city to see how they were disparaging homemakers is just one indication of how little respect is given to parents in the United States today. Indeed, families who value time together often find themselves swimming upstream against a cultural tide that says in countless ways that the needs of children are less important than the aspirations of adults.

Of course, some of the biggest obstacles to family togetherness in the 1990s have less to do with cultural attitudes than with economic conditions. For many of the families I know, the problem is not that Mom would get no respect if she were to leave her job to be home more with the kids or that Dad would be the butt of jokes if he were to take a less-demanding job so he could get home in time to coach Junior's Little League team. The problem, instead, is that many families just don't have the economic freedom to pursue what they regard as the best work/family arrangement. They feel trapped economically. Or they're just one paycheck away from a crisis.

Some feelings of economic pressure are the inevitable byproduct of parental responsibility and sacrifice. They're the types of pressures parents face in every generation, in good times and bad. These can be healthy pressures, for they can encourage stewardship, thrift, and unselfishness. Indeed, the sacrifices parents make for their children wouldn't be considered sacrifices if they were always easy.

But no civilization can long survive if it expects heroic acts to be routine. And in America today, it seems that heroic sacrifices are often required if parents are to meet their twin responsibilities of providing for their children's material needs and spending ample amounts of time to raise them well.

A VISION FOR A BETTER FUTURE

The America we seek, then, is one where a child's need for time with his or her parents is a top priority. It's an America where this priority is reflected in the private decisions parents make about meeting work and family responsibilities, and in the public policies that govern the tax treatment of families and the work options available to them.

In our America, family togetherness is prized, not as some far-off dream or utopian vision, but as an attainable goal for ordinary people willing to make ordinary sacrifices—for those who work hard and play by the rules.

The America we seek is not one in which everyone is compelled to adopt the same strategy for achieving family togetherness. Some families will want two earners; others will want just one. Some couples will want to work concurrent shifts; others will want to work split shifts so that one parent is almost always available to the children.

But the America we seek is one where families regularly eat meals together, take trips to see Grandma together, and do homework together. It's an America where parents get home from work with enough energy to throw a ball in the backyard, lead a Scout camp-out, or take a hot meal to the elderly shut-ins who live around the corner. The cultural elites of our country sometimes laugh at this vision. They derisively call it out of date and old-fashioned. This is the America of Ozzie and Harriet, they claim, and it's gone forever. But as I travel around our country—in nearly every state in the last two years—I find that Americans yearn to reestablish those family ties.

The country we want to build would be one where the little Laura Sorrells will never have to be embarrassed for having parents who care enough to be there for them when they arrive home from school, when they skin their knees, or when they just want to talk to someone. And it's an America where marital commitments are taken seriously. Where those who walk away from their family responsibilities are held financially accountable. Where men and (especially) women do not fear that investments in family life could leave them vulnerable to poverty should their spouses abandon them.

POLICY RECOMMENDATIONS

What sorts of public policies are needed to make this dream a reality?

1. First and foremost, families—especially families with dependent children—need massive tax relief. I'm not talking about a tax-cut plan that allows all Americans to keep a few more pennies from their paychecks. I'm talking about a tax cut that directs the lion's share of relief to families with children so that they can more easily make ends meet without abandoning their child-rearing responsibilities.

For too long, our nation's economic policies have ignored those trying to raise children. In 1948, a median-income family of four sent only two cents of every dollar to the federal government in income and payroll taxes. Today, a median-income family of four sends nearly a quarter of every dollar to Uncle Sam. And another dime, on average, goes to state and local government coffers. This tax burden is outrageous![1]

As you can imagine, this dramatic increase in the tax burden on families is one of the main reasons families today find it difficult to live on the average 40-hour-a-week wage. Yet the inability of parents to make ends meet on a 40-hour wage actually fuels the demand for more government. Indeed, many of the battles fought in Washington in recent years have been over things, like child care, that families once provided for themselves. Thus, cutting the family tax burden would not only make life easier for parents, but it would also reduce the demand for government programs that supplant families.

Federal and state policymakers can reduce the tax burden on families in several different ways. Some want to increase existing tax exemptions for children.

Others want to provide new tax credits for children. However it's done, the most important thing is that the tax code allow families to keep more of the money they earn and treat families with children differently from other taxpayers.

It's appropriate to permit a family of five making $45,000 a year to pay less tax than a single person making $45,000 a year, especially since most taxpayers will at some point be facing significant child-rearing expenses. Indeed, the best way to think of pro-family tax relief is that it's relief for people during that stage in life when their family responsibilities are greatest.

2. Promote economic growth. Per-child tax savings are not our sole concern. We believe that all Americans are overtaxed and that big government hinders the kind of economic growth that raises all boats on the sea of opportunity. We favor a decrease in the capital gains tax and lower marginal tax rates. Government should get out of the way and allow American entrepreneurship to take over. Growth equals jobs, and jobs are good for families.

Moreover, we recognize that the income-tax code is riddled with all sorts of inequities and perverse incentives, many of which threaten the social contract that has held our country together for more than two centuries. At a time when many working-class people who play by the rules are seeing long-term stagnation in real hourly wage rates, it is not only irresponsible but also potentially dangerous for government tax and welfare policies to continue to penalize socially responsible behavior like marriage and paid work.

A British member of Parliament has proposed an "anniversary tax cut" for married couples, beginning in the tenth year after marriage. Economists may question the idea, but the mortgage-interest deduction was based on the idea that home ownership makes for stable, productive communities. Is there any question that long-term marriages contribute even more to stability and productivity?

Thus, current tax and welfare policies that make it more financially attractive for couples to divorce or cohabit must be reversed. Similarly, policies surrounding the tax deductibility of contributions to an individual retirement account (IRA) should be altered so that homemakers can deduct as much as employed women. Moreover, efforts to simplify the entire tax code through some variation of a flat tax are certainly laudable, provided that the resulting code continues to significantly adjust tax liability for family size and for charitable contributions. Indeed, eliminating the tax deductibility of charitable contributions would undermine efforts to replace America's faltering welfare state with a vibrant charitable sector that meets more than just the material needs of America's poor.

3. In addition to pro-family tax relief, changes in the workplace policies of America's employers are needed. Specifically, employers should seek to give family-oriented workers greater discretion over when, where, and how much they work for pay. Where possible, arrangements that permit full- or part-time work from home ought to be encouraged. So should flexible work schedules, compressed work weeks, part-time work, and job sharing. The goal should not be to offer programs or services (such as on-site day care) that employers perceive some families may need but instead to give family-oriented workers the ability to meet their unique needs in the way that works best for them. This not only argues for flexible work arrangements, but also for flexible forms of compensation (more cash wages!) instead of rigid employee benefits that serve the interests of only a narrow range of employees.

Indeed, many companies have adopted "cafeteria" benefit plans that allow employees to pick and choose from an array of options. Some employees select dental benefits, others opt for greater leave time, and still others choose educational assistance. Whatever the choices, decision making is put in the hands of the employee, and benefits are tailored to meet the needs of his or her life stage and family circumstances.

4. Divorce reform is desperately needed. Advocates who brought us no-fault divorce in the 1970s promised a country of wanted marriages. They've given us a land that favors those who don't want marriage.

Today, it's easier to break this most sacred of contracts than it is to get out of a contract to have your lawn fertilized. In 1960, there were only 390,000 divorces.[2] Today, of the more than one million divorces granted each year, three-fifths involve couples with children under the age of 18.[3]

Our recent FRC survey showed that 94 percent of Americans believe children suffer because of divorce,[4] and the American people are right. According to researcher Judith Wallerstein, divorce is almost always more damaging, its effects more lasting, for children than for their parents. The harm is not simply psychological, something to be "treated" by friendly lectures by Barney the dinosaur. In fact, Wallerstein found, children of divorced parents generally receive less attention, undergo less discipline, suffer worse health, display more antisocial behavior, and suffer from more emotional and sexual problems than youths raised in intact families. Not surprisingly, they also have a more negative outlook on life.[5]

A 1987 poll of youngsters found that four out of 10 children from ages eight to 17 say that one of their worst fears is that their parents will divorce.[6] *USA Today* found that 54 percent of adults think divorce should be more difficult to obtain—and 76 percent of children agree! Three out of four of those children also think most couples who have divorced might have tried harder to save their marriages.[7] The kids are right on all counts!

Divorce does more than immediate harm, too. It also extends the damage into the future, virtually guaranteeing a host of problems for years to come. Children raised in divorced families, according to a 1992 Auburn University study, typically view marriage less favorably than their peers.[8] That this is not just opinion was demonstrated by Dr. Silvio Silvestri, who found that female children of divorce are five times more likely to go through a divorce themselves than women raised in intact families. Men raised in divorced households are three times more likely to suffer marital breakdown than those from intact families.[9]

We can change this by returning to a covenant idea of marriage. A *covenant*, according to George Mason University family-law expert Margaret Brinig, "is an especially solemn type of contract, one that cannot be broken without significant penalties." Such a contract is not merely an agreement between two individuals but a "promise under seal" of the state or of God Himself. A covenant idea would move much closer to allowing couples to make a legally binding lifelong commitment to family life.[10] We can shore up marriage with legal safeguards and enforceable periods for reflection and reconciliation. One thing is clear: No society can afford a succession of Me generations. We have a right, as well as a duty, to call people to consider the well-being of their children.

5. Increase family wages. In the last 20 years, "free trade" has been a central plank of the conservative revolution. I worked for a free-trade president, and I support the concept of open markets. But no policy position should go unquestioned, and I find myself asking whether the free-trade mantra is being used to play American families for suckers.

One of my most vivid childhood memories is of my father coming home one night and crying at our kitchen table because he had lost his blue-collar job. He was a proud man, and he defined his purpose on earth by his job and his ability to provide for his family. How many other families have witnessed the same scene because a breadwinner's job has been undercut by slave or sweatshop labor halfway around the globe? I don't want a trade war, but we shouldn't be a party to a trade surrender, either. Our trading partners must open their markets to our goods. Moreover, a 10 percent tariff on imports from Japan would raise $12 billion a year, which could be used to eliminate taxes on small businesses, which are overwhelmingly family enterprises.[11]

In a pro-family America, politicians would remember that working men and women who play by the rules have kept this country going. They deserve more than cold rhetoric about "efficient markets" and "new paradigms." Too often, our system seems to tilt toward multinational corporations that don't even think of themselves as American companies anymore—or toward the welfare class. Lost between the cracks are the middle-class and working-class families that make our country strong.

6. Congress should adopt legislation requiring that the "family impact" of a bill be assessed before it's considered on the floor of the House or Senate. Before a new housing project or dam goes up, the law requires that the agencies involved file an environmental impact statement on its foreseeable effects. On September 2, 1987, President Reagan issued an executive order requiring that "the autonomy and rights of the family" be "considered in the formulation" of federal policies and regulations. Congress (and even the states) should take similar measures to ensure that bills on everything from crime to welfare to tax reform

have been analyzed to determine their consequences
for families before they become law.

✦ ✦ ✦

Questions for Those Who Would Lead Us

1. Will you work for family tax relief that takes the
   costs of child rearing into account?
2. Will you support reform of so-called no-fault
   divorce to provide additional safeguards for
   covenant marriage?
3. Will you support a flat tax in which dependent
   deductions and charitable contributions are
   protected?
4. Will you work to give homemakers the same tax
   advantages of IRAs currently enjoyed only by
   those working outside the home?
5. Will you support "cafeteria plans" that offer
   employees higher wages rather than such
   restricted benefits as on-site day care?
6. Will you work to protect American workers from
   competition by slave laborers in China and elsewhere? Will you also alert consumers to abusive
   labor practices in Central American countries and
   elsewhere that produce goods for the U.S. market?

✦ 7 ✦

In the Name of Fairness

As I've mentioned, for the first time in our history, adults believe that life in this country will be worse, not better, for their children than it is for them. That belief is not mere fear: Signs of decline are everywhere. We're not yet in free fall, but we are rolling downhill, gathering terrible momentum. One reason is that our nation is no longer a level playing field. Millions of Americans no longer believe that life in our nation is fair.

It's not just the "haves" who express this sense that something is deeply out of balance, either. Even many beneficiaries of government aid know it. They see welfare policy failing the most basic test: Their welfare is deteriorating. Not long ago, Alex Kotlowitz of the *Wall Street Journal* wrote a powerful book about inner-city Chicago called *There Are No Children Here*. Kotlowitz recounted a conversation with a 10-year-old named Lafayette Rivers who lived in one of Chicago's vast public-housing projects. "I asked Lafayette what he wanted to be," Kotlowitz wrote. "'If I grow up,' the boy said, 'I'd like to be a bus driver.'"[1]

The word *if* in Lafayette's answer broke my heart. This 10-year-old, an American boy only a year older than my own son, Zachary, wasn't sure he would ever make it to adulthood. The hopelessness infused in his response to the most routine question every adult asks a child tells us without doubt that our welfare system has failed. However high the barriers to success were at Lafayette's birth, they seem higher now.

In this world, most of us never make it to that "shining city on a hill" where our dreams are realized. But at least we can see it, and most of us—most Americans, at least—bathe in the light of what the world considers luxury. But to Lafayette Rivers, that light must look far away and unreachable. Poverty may have erected the first wall around his life, but hopelessness has completed the other walls and the ceiling.

Is there no way out of such gross unfairness? Harvard's Robert Coles believes there is at least one. He wrote about Ruby Bridges, the six-year-old girl who launched the integration of the New Orleans public-school system in the 1960s. Against the mob hatred she faced, plus the burden of family poverty and illiteracy, how did she overcome? Coles says the best explanation lies in the "religious tradition" of Ruby's family.[2]

Coles's observation could be applied to the downtrodden of every race and society. It is the foremost unfairness of our time that religious ideals—the very ones that undergird our system of law and foster the conditions of success for the deprived—are the ideals most often mocked by our media and political culture.

Welfare policy in the United States, for example, was once the churches' responsibility. The American way of compassion used to be one-to-one help, not an anonymous check distributed by harried bureaucrats.

Today's civil libertarians ignore the progressive breakdown of the family that has come with expansion of the welfare state. Trying to use government authority to hamstring tax-supported church social agencies—covering over crucifixes, eliminating religious references in their materials, and forcing them to forsake all mention of their basic moral teachings—has been their rule of thumb.

In 1989, for example, the original version of the Act for Better Child Care included strict language against religious activity in any child-care center that received even a penny of public funds. Religious symbols would have to be covered, religious references in brochures deleted, and lunchtime prayers prohibited.[3] In February 1994, a federal Housing and Urban Development official told Family Research Council that religiously oriented nursing homes "should consider a vote to change their name" in order to satisfy the sectarian requirements of the Fair Housing Act of 1989.[4]

A VISION FOR A BETTER FUTURE

In the America we envision, citizens would look to their hearts again, not to the statehouses or faraway Washington, to address the needs of their neighbors. In the America we desire, welfare would not be an anonymous exchange of cash but an interplay of personal charity. In our America, churches, synagogues, and other private charities would once again be the agencies of first resort for families in need, with government providing assistance only in cases of genuine emergency.

In this America, a decision to marry would not be economically penalized at any income level. Deadbeat dads would be scorned, but so, too, would the wealthy absentee dads who pay up but starve their children for love. The high roller who puts away a devoted wife of 30 years for a "trophy spouse" would face the same social ostracism as the truck driver who flees cross-country, leaving a woman single and pregnant. In our America, welfare grants would not increase for each child born out of wedlock, but ultimately money is not the issue: No one would lionize the Murphy Browns of the world who willfully conceive a child knowing it will be fatherless.

Charles Augustus Ballard, founder and president of the National Institute for Responsible Fatherhood and Family Development, puts the need for a father as well as a mother bluntly:

Look at the social pathologies that plague us today: drug abuse, homicide, gang violence, crime. Now among the youth who fall prey to any or all of these calamities, ask them where their father was when their lives took a turn for the worse. Or visit our prisons and ask the men locked up what role their father played in their lives. You'll find too many who say, "No role at all."[5]

Seventy percent of all juveniles in our long-term correctional facilities did not grow up with their fathers in the household.[6] A three-year study of psychiatric admissions to two New Orleans hospitals in the *Journal of the American Academy of Child and Adolescent Psychiatry* found that nearly 80 percent of the preschool admittees came from fatherless homes.[7]

In our America, work would not be seen as a "penalty" the impoverished must endure in order to gain a benefit. Rather, work would be seen as the door through which individuals push their talents to improve their families, their neighborhoods, and their country. Any honest labor should be a source of pride as well as sustenance.

POLICY RECOMMENDATIONS

What principles must we follow to make welfare policy both fair and pro-family? The following come from various sources.

1. No one accepting public assistance should be better off than anyone dutifully paying his or her taxes. This seems self-evident, but the most damaging effects of welfare are the advantages it confers on people who choose the public dole over an entry-level job. Liberal social critics speak derisively of jobs "flipping burgers" or pushing a donut cart. But the tragedy is not that so many jobs like those are routine, because all work is sometimes routine, and all work has worth. The tragedy is that our system of welfare makes routine work an irrational choice for young men and women who can "earn" more by idleness. Reforms like the expansion of the Earned Income Tax Credit, which was adopted with pro-family support, have aided the working poor with children, but the rationality of welfare over work persists.

One look at the insane incentives of welfare is convincing. To match the value of welfare benefits, a Cato Institute study says, a mother with two children would have to earn at least $36,400 if she lives in Hawaii. In New York, Massachusetts, Connecticut, the District of Columbia, Alaska, Rhode Island—and, of course, Hawaii—welfare pays more than a $12.00-per-hour job, more than two and a half times the minimum wage. In 40 states, it pays more than an $8.00-an-hour job.[8]

The longer it remains true that Americans can improve their lot by going on welfare, the sooner we will reach a point where the whole system breaks down. Welfare must be reformed so that a decision to work is always more economically rewarding than a decision to watch.

Reducing welfare benefits is one way to reach this goal. Measures to restore the U.S. manufacturing base are another. One cause of the "feminization of poverty" has been the "demasculinization" of America's industrial centers. While paper and steel mills close here at home, our foreign-aid dollars help to subsidize expansion of those industries overseas. Weakening the opportunities of male providers, especially minorities, has exacted a terrible price.[9]

Enhancing the incentives for work and marriage provided by the Earned Income Tax Credit would be a third way to make a job more appealing than welfare.

2. All able-bodied recipients without young dependent children must work. We've put on blinders about the messages that prevail in most of our cities. I'm not talking about the messages of street life, but the messages from government. The twin pillars of the lottery window and the welfare office convey the idea that the American ideal is "something for nothing," and that the only way to get ahead is by the luck of the draw.

Having to work to receive welfare benefits is not a punishment but the benefit. The closer the life of the welfare recipient comes to the life of the workaday citizen, the sooner that recipient will take steps to upgrade his or her skills and compensation. A number of experiments are under way across the country to accelerate the welfare-to-work transition. They involve both public- and private-sector jobs. The key is that these jobs are mandatory and require real work. If you accept the community's help to provide you with food and shelter, it's no punishment to expect you to help the community in return.

3. Three decades of welfare trends make it clear: Washington does not know best. The only significant welfare activity taking place at the federal level today is the system of granting "waivers" so that states can devise and test their own ideas for dealing with poverty. The national government has become a gate-keeper, maintaining the status quo and granting exceptions like a bored Caesar. Experiments in work-fare and wedfare, efforts to put churches and communities back on the front line in the antipoverty fight—all are inspired by leadership in places like Trenton, Madison, and Jackson, not Washington. It's time that federal bureaucrats backed away and became students again, evaluating the laboratories of the states and giving the nation an annual "lab report" on welfare reform.

4. Welfare policy must cease rewarding bad behaviors and resume rewarding good ones. A live-in boyfriend who marries a welfare mother typically costs her and her children thousands of dollars in benefits.[10] A young mother on welfare who has another child out of wedlock increases hers. As has been said by others, "There are only two rules for getting welfare in America. First, you may not work, and second, you may not be married to anyone who does." Avoiding work and marriage is a risky strategy even for people of means; for impoverished people, it may be economically fatal.

After three decades of the War on Poverty, marriage is still the primary route out of dependency for welfare recipients. The cultural attack on marriage has had profound economic impact on the United States via welfare policy alone. Creative policy change is needed. Suppose, for instance, that instead of increasing cash benefits with the birth of an additional illegitimate child, a state used that same money to establish a personal savings account that a welfare recipient could tap only if she married and only to make a down payment on a first home. Our policies must communicate clearly: It's not the money we begrudge you; it's the chronic behavior that makes our monetary help futile.

5. If you have come to the United States illegally, expect only that help which is necessary to sustain you on your trip back home. The poem by Emma Lazarus that adorns our Statue of Liberty speaks of a Golden Door. It does not speak of climbing through broken windows. Those who enter our country legally—heirs of our proud and generous immigrant tradition—should find us a welcoming nation. But those who "break and enter" the United States, making their first act on our soil defiance of the law, should find their stay as pleasant as it is short.

The U.S. Census Bureau estimates that there are some four million illegal immigrants now residing in the United States, and that about 300,000 more settle here permanently every year.[11] This is a national scandal. How can we tell Americans to "play by the rules and you'll get ahead" when we tax them to confer public benefits on people who haven't played by the rules?

6. Religious and private charities must take the leading role again in solving poverty in all its dimensions. As historian Marvin Olasky has pointed out, social change in pre–Great Society America was primarily the work of volunteers who took on the "narrow but deep responsibility" of making a difference in another person's life over several years.

Modern welfare policy is, in contrast, wide but shallow. Real welfare reform must include ideas to increase personal charity, fostering not just notions of self-help but also ideals of neighbor help. Expanding tax deductions for charitable contributions is one way to move toward this goal.

✦ ✦ ✦

This chapter has focused on the fundamental unfairness the welfare system perpetuates. But welfare may be only a small part of the reason most Americans see the deck as stacked against the responsible and law-abiding citizen. They see a nation in which:

✦ Parents are told they are responsible for their children's education, yet they're denied, or have taxed away, the resources to provide that education.

✦ Entrepreneurs and job creators are tied up in bureaucratic red tape and penalized for their achievements, while billions of tax dollars go to special-interest groups. Subsidies for everything from ethanol and corn sweetener to mohair and timber harvesting cost taxpayers some $85 billion in fiscal year 1995 alone. The federal budget contains some 125 subsidy programs of this kind.[12]

✦ Qualified building contractors with the lowest bids are denied the opportunity to work on certain government projects, not because of the quality of their work, but because of the color of their skin.

✦ Media violence and explicit sex have free access to our homes, while God is barred from our schools.

✦ Bills adopted by elected bodies that passed, or would have passed, constitutional muster for centuries are overturned by unelected judges dedicated to imposing results that reflect their own pet theories.

✦ If you're a working family, you postpone having a child until you can afford one, while third-generation welfare recipients have children or abort them at taxpayer expense.

✦ If you're a celebrity, you can buy justice; if you're a millionaire, you can spend unlimited amounts of money on a candidate so long as that candidate is yourself; if you're wealthy and anti-school-choice, you can pay to keep your children out of the public schools to which your policies channel everyone else.

✦ If you're a victim of crime, your best hope of restitution is suing to recover money the criminal earned by selling the story of what he or she did—or claims not to have done—to you.

✦ If you run off with your best friend's wife, you'll be lionized by the cameras. If you remain your wife's best friend, you'll be told you hark back to "good old days" that were never really good.

It's been written that America is great because America is good, and that if America ever ceased to be good, it would also cease to be great. To that I would add that if we don't redress these examples of unfairness, we will cease to be free.

✦ ✦ ✦

Questions for Those Who Would Lead Us

1. Will you support a system of welfare in which those who depend on the community for help are required in return to help the community?
2. Will you support a "family cap" (i.e., no increase in cash benefits for unwed mothers who bear an additional child while already on welfare) to help restore the social consensus that out-of-wedlock childbearing is wrong at any income level?
3. Will you work for restrictions on welfare benefits to illegal aliens?
4. Will you require all able-bodied welfare recipients without young dependent children to work?
5. Will you return welfare to local governments and community organizations?
6. Will you take steps to reduce U.S. contributions to such entities as the Export-Import Bank that in turn subsidize the creation and growth of foreign competitors with U.S. manufacturers? What other steps will you take to build our industrial base for the benefit of primary wage earners?

✦ 8 ✦

Schools That
Teach Again

Some of the most vivid memories of my childhood are those evenings when my father would come home after 12 or 13 hours of working, covered with the grime and dirt of his blue-collar job. He would limp through the house, favoring the leg he injured as a marine in the South Pacific, a leg he would eventually lose to gangrene. Then, grabbing me by the arms and insisting that I look at him good and hard, he would describe one more time why studying and learning were my ticket to avoiding the dead-end jobs in which he was stuck. Dad had dropped out of high school to get his family through the Great Depression.

Don't get me wrong. There's nothing inferior about working with your hands. It's noble work compared with the paper-pushing jobs so common in Washington, D.C. I spent one summer loading 50-pound mail sacks on trucks at the Disabled American Veterans headquarters. That was work my father understood, and he was proud of me. But he was trying to guarantee me something better and more reliable than the heavy-industry jobs on which the Midwest economy depended.

There was nothing unique about that scene in my childhood home. It has been played out in household after household, from the early days of the republic until now. Schooling in the United States has always been seen as the way one generation could reach the higher plane that was out of reach for its mothers and fathers. But in the last 30 years, the American educational enterprise has tottered near collapse. The trend lines since 1962 are strikingly clear. Math and verbal scores began their relentless downward slide, while per-pupil spending on education maintained its relentless climb.[1]

In too many cities, for too many of our children, our schools are no longer working. The problems are both wide and deep. Only one-third of the nation's high school seniors are proficient readers, down another 10 percent in just two years.[2] Violence is rampant. Sixty percent of urban schools responding to a National School Boards Association survey in 1993 reported student assaults on teachers.[3] Roughly 135,000 guns are brought into schools every day.[4] The United States spends a higher percentage of its gross national product on education than do Germany, Japan, South Korea, France, Great Britain, and other countries, yet it lags them all in educational outcomes.[5] We can and must do better if the American dream is going to survive.

A VISION FOR A BETTER FUTURE

Here's the educational system our pro-family movement seeks to build: Our schools would be safe again. No longer would our children and their teachers have to fear assault by young thugs or gangs. We know learning can't take place unless there's a sense of security.

The schools would focus on the basics. The public, year after year, says it wants the schools to teach children to read, write, and do math correctly. Schools that can't accomplish that for all their students are failing, and we would close them.

Our school day would begin with the Pledge of Allegiance again, a ceremony that in too many school districts has already disappeared. There would also be a moment for students to exercise their religious liberty by prayer or reflection and to recognize the God who has given us liberty.

In the American educational system we want to build, there would be no need for longer school days and a longer school year. We know the problem is not a lack of time in class. The problem is that the time our children spend there is all too often being wasted by bureaucracy and frivolity. Our schools would be built around the simple notion that parents are the first and most important teachers a child has. The school official who doesn't understand this basic fact should be in another line of work.

We would make sure schools were regularly rated and teachers regularly tested for competency. Parents should know which schools are working and which aren't. They should know which teachers have subject mastery and which don't. Our schools would be built on a simple principle captured in a simple question: "What works?" Unfortunately, too much of what works has been forgotten in American education; fads have replaced tried-and-true methods. We would put those methods back in the center of the educational enterprise.

Our schools would have high expectations of all students, regardless of race or economic background. All our students can achieve if the adults in their lives will fulfill their responsibilities and hold the kids to high standards.

Cutting back the school bureaucracy will inevitably free up money to ensure that our teachers are paid a decent and living wage. For example, the Catholic schools of Washington, D.C., have 50,000 students but a central administration of only 17 people. In contrast, the D.C. public-school system has 81,000 students with a central administration of 1,500 employees.[6] And easing the pressures from a bloated central administration and empowering teachers to design their own curricula were the keys to turning around the East Harlem School District in New York City.[7]

We would also dismantle the educational establishment and fire the busybody bureaucrats in Washington, D.C. The idea that 10,000 government employees at the federal Department of Education know better how to run the schools of Cincinnati, Denver, or Sacramento is an anachronism that no longer makes sense as Americans strive to retain more power in their own communities.

A graduate of our schools would know things like who wrote the Declaration of Independence and what makes it unique; what happened at Concord's North

Bridge, Antietam, and on the beaches of Normandy; and what relevance these places have for the lives of modern children. They would know who said, "Give me liberty or give me death," and who said, "I have a dream." As Bill Bennett has suggested, all our children should know what such places as Constitution Hall look like and what good music sounds like.

In short, our schools would be dedicated to teaching our children to love the things we love and honor the things we honor. All this and more are possible for American education.

POLICY RECOMMENDATIONS

American schools have been in decline for at least 30 years. In spite of increased spending, more "experts," and wave after wave of supposed reform, fewer children are getting the basic education they need to compete in the world and defend our values. We can and must do better.

1. Our children must be taught American history. Recent studies show that all too many 17-year-olds are woefully uninformed about their own country's history and literature, as well as those of other peoples. A test of 22,000 American seniors conducted for the National Assessment of Educational Progress (NAEP) and released in November 1995 found that 57 percent do not reach even the "basic" level of history knowledge. Only 39 percent chose Abraham Lincoln as the author of a familiar quotation on slavery from his famous "house divided" speech.

(This was a multiple-choice question, so 25 percent should have answered correctly if they had merely guessed!)[8] And many seniors can't identify the half century in which the Civil War occurred.[9]

The NAEP joins a long line of surveys and reports making it clear that, in spite of spending billions in tax dollars on schooling, our education system is graduating young Americans who don't have the basic facts about our nation's past. We shouldn't be surprised. For years, major textbooks have been leaving out essential facts. Check your son's or daughter's American history books, or consult the 1994 National History Standards project (a two-year effort to decide what every child should know about the U.S.). In the latter, you'll find no mention of many of the heroes who made our country great—Paul Revere, Robert E. Lee, Thomas Edison, Jonas Salk, and the Wright brothers, to name a few. The standards mention Madonna and Roseanne but omit Marian Anderson, Margaret Chase Smith, and Mother Seton.[10] One textbook left out such giants as Ethan Allen, Nathan Hale, John Paul Jones, and George Washington Carver but found space to devote to Bob Dylan, Janis Joplin, and Joan Baez.

But if only the holes in American education were mere facts!

Facts are useful only insofar as they serve as windows on the past. The child who lacks those windows will never be able to peer into a time other than his or her own. Here in Washington, a street corner near my office offers one such window. It's an ordinary intersection of busy roads, Vermont and L Streets, bounded by tall office buildings and choked with traffic at nearly every hour of the day. But there are facts about this corner through which glimpses of what matters most about this nation can be caught. Here the poet Walt Whitman observed President Lincoln pass nearly every day in the hot summer of 1863. "I saw very plainly," he wrote in the *New York Times*, "the President's dark brown face, with the deep cut lines, the eyes, &c, always to me with a deep latent sadness in the expression."[11]

I love pointing out such places to my children. All our children must be reminded of their roots and the sacrifices that were made by brave men and women. Every acre of this land of ours has some resonance of meaning, from Mount Katahdin to Catalina Island. An education that does not give every American child a sense of this meaning is a betrayal. This betrayal encompasses not just the giants of long ago, but also the giants of recent times, and the more mundane. It encompasses the North Bridge at Concord, Massachusetts, where "the shot heard round the world" was fired, and a bridge over the Alabama River in Selma where a band of civil rights marchers made a similar stand for freedom.

It encompasses thousands of other bridges, factories, and farms as well where, so far as I know, no acts of extraordinary heroism occurred but where ordinary workers gave their sweat and muscle to build a better way for their families. This is heroism, too, though we have ceased to recognize it.

Our national Revolutionary and Civil War

battlefields should be protected from overdevelopment. I generally side with free-enterprise conservatives, but these places are what Lincoln called "this hallowed ground." We don't live by bread alone. When we bulldoze our past, we're in danger of burying our national heritage.

Every acre of this land of ours has been repurchased time and again with the blood, sweat, and tears of patriots and families. It's scandalous for our children not to know the calendar dates of the pivotal events in the history of our nationhood. But it's a tragedy for the meaning of those dates to be invisible to the minds of our children.

This national amnesia won't be reversed by more reliance on the education bureaucrats in Washington, either. Two million dollars of our tax money were spent for the National History Standards project. What did we get for our money? Hundreds of pages of "politically correct" pap that, in addition to the oversights I mentioned earlier, omitted any reference to Daniel Webster, Albert Einstein, or even Martha Washington.

Worst of all, these anti-American history standards wanted all young Americans to know about "Soviet advances in space" and the Challenger disaster, but they failed to point out that the United States landed the first men on the moon. Those academics and bureaucrats should have used some of that $2 million to go see *Apollo 13*. They might have noticed that American audiences actually applaud that heartwarming story of heroism and dedication.

2. Our children must know, too, the special character of the nation, and they must be taught that it's good. The United States has made mistakes, and those shouldn't be glossed over, but the current hostility to our country and its past that permeates so many textbooks and too many schools is wrong and must be rejected.

Some will say this is self-evident. Others will say it's jingoistic. But I say that the evidence of history is clear. In the last two decades, just as American educators and textbook publishers began to toss overboard any references to the United States as a triumphant nation, the rest of the world flocked to the model our Founders gave them! The people of Eastern Europe huddled around contraband radios to hear our broadcasts of world news, and the students of Tienanmen Square built a model of the Statue of Liberty and paraded it in the streets. But here at home, our elites all too often deride as "flag wavers" anyone who dares to say this nation is special.

In 1994, the Lake County, Florida, school board was barraged with derisive headlines and scathing editorials in the press. What was its sin? The board had adopted a resolution requiring that students "acquire an appreciation of our American heritage and culture."[12] In many cases, the critics did not merely believe that the Lake County board was being inappropriately boastful. They thought it was wrong to suggest that America's culture and values are better than those of other nations. Unfortunately, Lake County was stung by this national criticism and retreated. The real tragedy is that when that board said what previous generations of Americans uniformly believed, it caused such a firestorm.

More county and state school boards should pass resolutions like that adopted by Lake County. More important, we need to have enough confidence in our values, history, and philosophy of free government to want to teach them to all children. If we have no public ethos, why do we need public education?

An education that can't address bedrock ethics is not worthy of the name "American." Our schools and our children must understand: To be a force for good in the world requires first that we be good citizens of the United States, good citizens of our towns and neighborhoods, and good members of our families. Patriotism is an honorable trait for the citizen of any country, even one whose government is seriously off course, but patriotism in this land is justice.

Sadly, millions of men and women today are detached from what T.S. Eliot called "the permanent things," bending with the latest wind, unfamiliar with the problems, solutions, and achievements of previous generations. They are prey to the passions of the moment—even the passions of tyrants and empty orators. The goal of education is to increase the endowment of the American people, and that begins, above all, with the same recognition that motivated our Founders: that every human being's endowment comes from the Creator.

3. Teach our children to read and write correctly. A host of educational fads in recent years has resulted in our forgetting the obvious in education—math, science, grammar, spelling, and the ability to express yourself still matter, even in an age of computers. Schools that have abandoned the phonetics approach to reading are beginning to recognize the disaster this decision has wrought. California, for example, instituted "whole language" reforms in 1987 that pushed phonics to the periphery of early education.[13] And California recently placed *last* in a national evaluation of reading skills among elementary-school students.[14]

Moreover, schools that regularly insist on homework do better than schools that don't. A recent study of California third-graders affirmed once again that high-achieving students are more likely than their peers to spend time on homework.[15]

The federal government continues to spend millions of our tax dollars trying to figure out "what works" in education. But it's trying to rediscover the obvious. Stop anyone on the streets of our major cities and ask what our schools should do. The answers are simple and consistent—less bureaucracy, higher standards, more homework, and regular testing. We already know what works; we just have to find the will to reinstitute the basics.

We must never make the mistake of confusing the basic with the simplistic. Some of the most earnest education reformers believe their methods are designed to introduce children to the complexity of learning—to get away from the deplorable fundamentals to which earlier generations were subjected. Nothing could be further from the truth. *Today's* methods tend toward the insipid. One glance at the materials used to educate young children in earlier times, such as *The Art of Penmanship* and *The New England Primer*, demonstrates not only that moral education was a constant aim, but also that even the youngest learners were presented with challenging subject matter.

As Boston University president and author John Silber points out, children just learning to write long-hand were asked to copy over many times such sentences as "Religion conduces to our present as well as our future happiness."[16] Imagine a first-grade class today presented with a comparable text. It isn't necessary to expose infants to flash cards and other "guaranteed genius" schemes. But once children exhibit their natural readiness to learn, the material we give them should be genuinely stimulating—real literature, not "Dick and Jane" monotony—not even "Jane and Dick" monotony to conform to feminist orthodoxy. The truth is that most such methods underestimate all our children.

4. Schools should get back to the basic task of teaching and reject socially and "politically correct" agendas and fads. Haven't we had enough of fads? Just recall the foolishness that has penetrated our classrooms in the last 20 years. Values clarification stripped actions bare of ethical content and encouraged students to supply their own meaning. The self-esteem movement told the young to value themselves, not as children of God with the duty to discover and develop their hidden talents, but as some kind of unique expression of the genetic code, with no particular responsibility to anyone but themselves. Outcome-based education stressed the kind of negotiating skills that no doubt made Neville Chamberlain (the British prime minister who kowtowed to Hitler) an A student. The feminist and ecological fads permeated and distorted the 1994 National History Standards, as seen above. All these things have been enthusiastically embraced by the federal education bureaucracy and the so-called "experts" who are prepared to embrace everything other than traditional education.

5. Parents must be restored to the center of the American educational experience. Parents are the first and most important teachers a child has. However, too much of the educational establishment regards parents as beside the point or a nuisance. This basic fact ought to inform all education officials: "You work for taxpaying parents." My daily mail contains heartbreaking stories of parents ignored, abused, and ridiculed by the educational establishment. Parents who object to book selections and curriculum decisions should be treated with respect, often heeded, and always accommodated regarding their own children. Schools should cease to be arenas where, as has happened in school districts from Falmouth, Massachusetts, to Toccoa, Georgia, condoms are foisted upon children without parental knowledge.[17]

Before children become hardworking citizens, they observe (or fail to observe) individuals they love engaged in the tasks of citizenship. Before they can read, they see a father reading daily to understand his world or carry out his job. Before they know the meaning of the word *duty*, they observe duty daily carried out by a mother who ignores her own well-being and places her children first.

We must honor parents in education, because, confused as things are today, most parents still give their children these role models at home. The most direct way to accomplish this goal is the Parental Rights Amendment, an idea promoted by a group calling itself Of the People. This proposal would amend state constitutions to include this simple and powerful statement: "The right of parents to direct the upbringing and education of their children shall not be infringed." This language expresses the everyday sense of ordinary American families—we have gotten away from it, to our great loss.

6. Choice in education, by any and every means, must be vigorously pursued. It cannot be said more plainly: Parental choice in education is the American way. Parents choose where to live, what to feed their children, what church to belong to, what careers to follow, whom to call their friends. A system of financing that doesn't allow them to choose schools for their children is so out of kilter that one wonders how it ever came to exist in this free nation.

In the summer of 1995, the state supreme court of Wisconsin issued an order blocking poor parents in Milwaukee from using vouchers to send their children to religious schools. Attorneys for the American Civil Liberties Union (ACLU) brought the suit. The decision produced some images I'll never forget. One news photo showed an impoverished woman hugging her child and weeping at the loss of the voucher that promised him a better education. Another showed the jubilant ACLU attorneys relishing their courtroom triumph. Whose defeat were they celebrating?

Educational choice will not mean the end of the public schools. Those who argue it will, including the teachers' unions, are using fear to resist a needed reform. On the contrary, choice is more likely to be the public schools' salvation. It will force the worst of them to close and the best of them—for which parents already line up for miles and otherwise maneuver to see their children admitted—to expand. Serious and useful argument is under way about whether the best path to school choice is targeted vouchers, tax credits, charter schools, or some other approach. But for now, the bottom line is this: Any initiative that expands the range of education options to a larger group of citizens is worthy of support. School choice may be the most important pro-family reform of them all.

7. Religious values must be restored to their proper place of respect in our schools. Here some progress has been made. The "equal access" rights of religious groups, including student Bible clubs and the like, are now firmly established in law. But contradictions and confusion are still rampant, and practices never envisioned as unconstitutional by our Founders are still under a cloud. Such things as religious invocations, prayers before football games, voluntary student-led prayer, and the singing of hymns and carols during holiday recitals are regularly attacked and banned. These inhibitions on First Amendment freedoms and community traditions should be resolved once and for all by a Religious Liberty Amendment to the Constitution. Once again, it's a tragedy that we need to amend the Constitution to restore its original meaning on so basic an issue, but amend it we must.

8. What you can do in your own home: The American press likes to describe social movements in broad terms. Lately, the home-schooling movement has come in for a wave of attention, some of it unflattering, much of it obviously concerned about the "erosion" of traditional forms of teaching. But the truth is, not only is home-schooling the traditional form of teaching, but also *all* parents are engaged in the home education of their children.

Schools become the primary teachers of children only by parental neglect. Not only do parents perform tasks of education before children enter school and during summer breaks, but they do so every evening and weekend as well. Above all, they do so by their example, especially the habits of constant questioning and lifelong learning they instill in their offspring.

No matter how sophisticated computers become, reading skills will remain precious. Moreover, no matter how pervasive video becomes, listening skills will remain invaluable. A good way to combine the development of these skills is for parents to read to children daily. Every child can listen to and appreciate literature that's above his or her current grade level. Besides, the time spent reading and explaining a story to children is certain to be among their most treasured memories.

Here are several other ideas within the reach of every family:

✦ America has over 15,000 libraries. They vary in size and quality, but even the smallest possess over 20,000 books. Interlibrary loan systems make hundreds of thousands of books available to the typical borrower. Parents should accompany their children to the library regularly. They should familiarize themselves with what's on the shelves, paying special attention to the classics and older works so often neglected in today's classrooms and media.

✦ Use technology prudently, and only after basic skills are mastered. No computer will transform a poor writer into a good one or a lousy mathematician into a genius with numbers. But technology can help those who have acquired basic skills to produce superior written work and swifter mathematical results. The same is true for videos. Consumed in large quantities, without regard for quality, they can enthrall children, destroy their sense of reality, and waste eons of time. But church and family networks can use video technology to help parents manage viewing time and select only the highest-quality

products. Libraries are expanding their collections in this area, too, and parents should take
swift steps to educate themselves about their
holdings and help guide them to the best material, be it Shakespeare plays, the really-high-qual-
ity PBS productions, or educational videos.

✦ The real cradle of faith and freedom is in every
family's home. A furor arose in Kentucky in the
1980s over a court's decision to compel the
removal of the Ten Commandments from a
classroom wall. Like so many other court rulings
on religious issues, this one is full of ironies. A
frieze of "Moses the Lawgiver" hangs on the
wall of the chamber of the U.S. House of
Representatives, directly opposite the Speaker's
chair. If that's permissible, it's clear to me that
the law Moses gave—the Ten Commandments—
can hang on a public schoolhouse wall. But parents who believe this, as I do, must ask themselves, do these commandments hang anywhere
in plain view on our own household walls?

Is there a single patriotic portrait on our
walls? Any quotations from the three "P's" of
moral education—Paul, Proverbs, or the
Psalms? (Of course, as a Christian, I believe the
greatest moral teacher of all was Jesus.) Do our
children know who the Sullivan brothers were
and the significance of the grove of crab-apple
trees planted in their memory on the Capitol
grounds by the grateful people of Iowa? This is
not ancient history. Just recently, the U.S. Navy

commissioned a new ship dedicated to those five young men who served together in World War II aboard the USS *Juneau* and gave the last, full measure of devotion on a single day of battle.

Do our children know the history of bigotry—that it didn't begin or end with the Civil Rights Act of 1964? That it hasn't been confined to issues of race but has deep roots in ethnic and religious hatreds that persist today? Few schools are likely to assign children to read a biography of William Wilberforce or John Wesley, but parents can. At the end of the day, our children should know that religious zeal has been the wellspring of social reform. The rights and dignity of every person do not come from the hand of government but from the hand of God.

✦ Buy a television with a five-foot cord, and put it six feet from the nearest outlet. Television is a voracious consumer of children's attention and mental energy. Infants just learning to walk can master the on/off switch. How many profitable hours of family interaction have been lost forever because a television was idly turned on and a few hours were spent taking in video junk food? If it isn't worth the forethought of digging out an extension cord to plug the set in, a show probably isn't worth watching. A family truly dedicated to education will place the strictest possible limits on television viewing. Research now clearly shows an inverse relationship between TV viewing and academic achievement—as TV time goes up, grades go down![18]

✦ The United States has some of the finest museums in the world. Too many, sadly, are warehousing their basic collections and devising gimmicks to entertain rather than educate children. But museums remain one of the best educational bargains in the world, and here at home they encompass art, history, natural history, and literally thousands of other specialized fields. Most museums are underutilized. Children may protest, but nearly every child walks away from a museum visit with invaluable new knowledge. Once again, parents can lead the way.

Like so much else, the revolution in American education must begin at home. Well begun there, it's a revolution that won't be quenched. This is the revolution in education the pro-family movement yearns to see.

✦ ✦ ✦

Questions for Those Who Would Lead Us

1. Will you support parental choice of schools through tuition tax credits or vouchers?
2. Will you work for schools where the Pledge of Allegiance is recited each day?
3. Do you support a Religious Liberty Amendment to the Constitution to guarantee the right of students voluntarily to pray and of all Americans to express religious ideas in the public square?

4. Will you work for schools that teach American history without apology and assure that students know the sacrifices made by our ancestors for our liberty?
5. Will you support the right of teachers to teach without joining the National Education Association (NEA) or American Federation of Teachers (AFT)? (According to *Forbes* magazine, the NEA collects some $750 million in annual dues from all levels of the union. A significant portion of that money is spent on partisan political activity and efforts to oppose educational reforms ranging from parental choice to parental rights and limits on value-free sex education.[19])

✦ 9 ✦

Toward a Culture of True Freedom

In many world capitals, blue jeans have become the symbol of American culture. Relaxed but rugged, friendly but fashionable, American jeans have come to stand for our way of life. Students from Prague to Seoul to Moscow would hand over a month's wages to buy a piece of American fabric. And what has happened in our "blue jeans culture" lately tells us a lot about what has happened to our way of life.

In the summer of 1995, the trendsetting Calvin Klein company unveiled a series of television and print ads that left even liberal media critics aghast. The ads featured young men and women who were, by all physical appearances, children. They were photographed in stark light, in provocative poses, with sexual characteristics emphasized, and their underclothing peering through. The television ads went even further. In them, the "child models" were shown against dingy, anonymous backdrops suggestive of porn films. A male voice-over commented on the models' physiques and asked them leering questions. I first saw one ad in my den with my older daughter and, like parents all over the country, was profoundly disturbed.

As reporters dug into the ad campaign, they discovered the still photos were taken by porn photographer Stephen Meisel, best known for producing pop singer Madonna's book *Sex*. The voice-overs were the work of a man known as Mr. Leather whose previous claim to fame was hosting programs on New York City's homosexual porn channel. Calvin Klein, the darling of movie stars and the cultural elite, had launched a new blue-jeans campaign that took the themes of child porn into every American home. Klein ultimately bowed to public outrage and withdrew the campaign. But a week later, his ads running in major newspapers depicted a young female model over the caption "Rock your pants off!"

A few weeks later, jeans-maker Levi Strauss followed with an ad campaign whose clear message was "If you want something, steal it." The Levi's ads were placed in bus-stop carrels. Real jeans were placed under the display ads' Plexiglas. The company clearly expected (even desired) the jeans to be stolen, because under them was cleverly imprinted an outline of the jeans with the slogan "Apparently they were very nice pants!"

These campaigns illustrate the depth of America's cultural decline. Yes, both campaigns were halted under public pressure, but both companies certainly profited from their paid and unpaid publicity. What once would have been fatal missteps making these companies social outcasts, even bankrupts, are now social attractions that build notoriety and cash balances. To paraphrase one of Klein's earlier prurient slogans, nothing comes between him and his profits.

Was it for this that young Germans danced on the ruins of the Berlin Wall? Did the iron fences of apartheid drop to be replaced by images of basement walls against which young girls arch their backs for the delight of decadent fashion flacks? Our leaders tell us that cultural barriers must fall to the call of global markets. Is this what the expansion of the American cultural marketplace—our films, our books, our fashion—will mean worldwide?

A VISION FOR A BETTER FUTURE

What kind of American culture do pro-family conservatives envision? Liberal critics say we want an Ozzie and Harriet culture that never really existed. As I look at the coarseness of our culture and its decadent images, I must admit to feelings of nostalgia. The fact is, it wasn't that long ago when the worlds of art, film, fashion, and culture were—not by law but by common cultural consent—overwhelmingly family friendly. Bohemian culture existed. Greenwich Village existed. But we were not a global Greenwich Village.

The real myth is not that American culture was never "good" in the sense of portraying a guiding morality. The real myth is that it upheld moral ideals at the expense of becoming unrealistic and bland. Norman Rockwell painted idyllic scenes of American life, but it was also his brush that most movingly caught Ruby Bridges' lonely walk into an all-white school in Louisiana. Jimmy Cagney could play gangsters as rotten as any that fill the screen today, but his talent also brought to life the redemption of a life-long thug in *Angels with Dirty Faces*. On the verge of execution, Cagney's character selflessly pretended to be a coward for the sake of the impressionable young-sters who had wrongly seen him as a hero. Compare that image with today's scenes of remorseless villains, on the silver screen and in the blind alleyways of Los Angeles, who revel in wanton violence.

In the America we envision, art would be as cre-ative as *Citizen Kane*, as morally complex as John Ford's *The Searchers*, as innovative as *Fantasia*, and as capable of handling romantic intimacy as *The Best Years of Our Lives*. But we would no longer have the routine use of sex and violence to titillate and exploit us for a quick buck. In reaching this goal, Americans would not resort primarily to law, because the history of governmental involvement in culture has been not to rescue it but to poison it.

The American cultural explosion in the first half of this century operated under rules of voluntary self-restraint. Those rules must be revived. The role of government would be sharply restricted.

POLICY RECOMMENDATIONS

Here are six ways to rescue American culture from its drop into the abyss:

1. Producers of crass, exploitative material should

be shunned and shamed. No laws were brought to bear in 1995 when Time-Warner was hauled into the court of public opinion. The media giant, which has produced and distributed cultural sewage from Madonna's *Sex* to "gangsta rap" that glorifies the murder of police and the rape of women, reshuffled its music division and began looking to unload its most offensive label, Interscope Records. One Time-Warner critic made the point perfectly clear: This issue is "not about censorship; it's about citizenship."[1]

In the world we envision, officers of companies like Interscope wouldn't be able to go to restaurants without meeting the scorn of everyone from busboys to fellow diners. No one would hail them as pioneers of the First Amendment; they would be seen for what they are: Boss Tweeds of cultural corruption. A healthy America would have a sense of shame again.

2. A genuine feminization of culture would finally take root. Several years ago, female editors at Simon & Schuster balked at the publication of Bret Easton Ellis's ultra-violent *American Psycho*. Simon & Schuster dumped the book.[2] It was a rare act of self-restraint by a major cultural force, and it was unique in that it came from senior businesswomen angry about the mistreatment of their sex.

Let's be frank. The enterprises of sexual exploitation, with a handful of exceptions, are carried out by men for the entertainment of men. If the cries of outrage against domestic violence and exploitation in our culture mean anything, they should mean overwhelming pressure on the muck-makers to cease and desist.

The number of women on U.S. corporate boards is growing dramatically. If that growth means anything, it should mean an end to the packaging of women as playthings for male consumption and destruction.

3. Government should say to the arts: Stand on your own two pillars. Those pillars are skill and imagination. The history of government funding of the arts is littered with . . . litter. Great artists do not need subsidies. That's especially true in this age when instant communications mean there are no backwaters of artistic activity. But even if recognition doesn't come quickly to all good artists, that is neither government's concern nor a problem that it can possibly cure.

The reverse is true. An individual paid in advance by government to produce a work of art has lost his or her incentive to create something that finds a home in the human heart. Government will always need a limited amount of art to adorn public buildings and honor the dead. But those are precisely the kinds of art subject to commissioned design and juried competitions. As the Vietnam Veterans Memorial shows, such works needn't be dull and predictable, but by their nature they will always have quality and dignity. That should be the rule, not the exception.

4. Government must take steps that empower parents, not limit speech. The proposal to install microchips (the so-called V-chip) in new television sets deserves pro-family support, provided neither government nor the entertainment corporate giants play any role in determining which programs are screened by such devices. In addition, any V-chip technology must allow for other, private ratings classifications. For example, if the technology were available, an organization like Focus on the Family could develop such a ratings system to help parents block objectionable programming.

Technology rarely, if ever, supplies an answer to what is at root a moral problem. But moral renewal is unlikely to happen in a heartbeat. Government can and must intervene to strengthen the hand of parents in stemming the tide of cultural pollution flowing toward their homes.

5. **Laws against obscenity and indecency must be vigorously enforced, with the cooperation of our courts**. Liberal-activist claims to the contrary, the First Amendment to the Constitution has never been interpreted to protect obscene speech and depictions. Moreover, the Federal Communications Commission, which licenses the airwaves, has the mandate and the power to provide "safe harbors" to protect children from indecent broadcasting. These laws should be vigorously defended, explained, and enforced without apology. Congress should continue to move with haste to extend legal controls to computer porn and other new technologies that are being used to distribute obscene materials.

Our courts have often undercut the message of obscenity statutes, and law enforcement agencies can wink at the problem, as the Clinton administration did in 1993 until public pressure shamed it into taking action. More must be done. The president and the nation's governors should appoint judges at all levels who uphold the rule of law and recognize the distinction between illegal pornography and protected speech.

6. Public institutions should act first as conservators of culture, not as outposts of the avant-garde. Under the influence of liberal activists, groups like the American Library Association and People for the American Way have allied themselves with a form of First Amendment radicalism that would make books like *The Joy of Gay Sex* available to children in public libraries.[3] The refusal of many public institutions to play any reasonable role in support of parents has contributed to the fraying of all sense of community responsibility.

At the same time, too many of our public libraries are following our schools by "dumbing down" their collections to accommodate the dumbing down of education. This must stop. Public funds for these traditional cultural institutions should be spent first on assuring that material of proven intellectual quality and worth is purchased and maintained. One survey we did at Family Research Council showed that the great historic and literary classics are disappearing from the shelves of America's libraries.[4]

Albert Einstein's *Relativity*, perhaps the most important work of physics in the twentieth century, is missing from nearly half the nation's libraries outside the major cities. Isaac Newton on the laws of thermodynamics and Johannes Kepler on astronomy are even more rare, as are important books by such major writers as Sir Walter Scott, Tolstoy, Malraux, C.S. Lewis, and G.K. Chesterton.

A FINAL WORD

Cultural decay is usually a glacierlike process. "Combat zones" of strip joints and prostitution don't just appear overnight. Movie theaters that screened *Showboat* on Tuesday didn't just start screening *Showgirls* on Wednesday. Watching one decadent film may not turn an audience of beauties into beasts, but a culture that turns regular Saturday matinee fare from Cecil B. DeMille's *The Ten Commandments* into Bo Derek's *10* will inevitably evolve from high civility to crass depravity.

Glaciers become avalanches when the cultural force is gambling. With stunning speed, America's flirtation with gambling has blossomed into a $40 billion-a-year industry premised on the previously un-American concept of something-for-nothing. More Americans now go to gambling establishments than attend baseball games, the national pastime.

Gambling relies on a can-bet spirit. Sheer luck, not merit or hard work, determines the winners and (much more numerous) losers. The roots of this transformation of the American spirit are hard to assess. It may be that many Americans see their fellow citizens getting ahead by the spoils of litigation, affirmative action, or inheritance—all situations where merit matters little. Or perhaps it's that government officials, who are desperate for new sources of tax revenue and who have gone out of their way to disconnect morality and law, no longer protect citizens from vulnerabilities that have always been there. Either way, a crass materialism has overtaken good sense.

The only winners at gambling are the bosses who own the casinos. Fools and their money are soon parted. Prostitution, theft, and neglect of spouse and children spring up in the vicinity of roulette wheels almost overnight. Political corruption follows, as public officials become dependent on cash obtained by legalized larceny. Other, legitimate businesses in the neighborhood collapse. Embezzlement to feed gambling addictions rises.

For example, in the suburbs near Atlantic City, New Jersey, the original capital of East Coast casino gambling, property values decreased by $24 million after the casinos opened—and by another $11 million in more-distant suburbs.[5] In Atlanta, the arrival of casino gambling coincided with a decline in the number of restaurants in the community from 243 to 146 between 1977 and 1987.[6] Robert Goodman, a professor at the University of Massachusetts, Amherst, has documented similar negative impacts in other communities where gambling has prospered.[7]

The collateral crimes associated with gambling are large. The Florida Department of Law Enforcement opposed legalized casinos in the state, finding that "casinos will result in more Floridians being robbed, raped, assaulted, and otherwise injured."[8] Seventeen South Carolina legislators were convicted several years ago of taking bribes to legalize horse and dog racing. Six Arizona legislators pled guilty in 1990 to accepting bribes in connection with a bill to legalize casinos. Seven Kentucky legislators pled guilty to the same offense the same year. In West Virginia, both a former governor and a state lottery director were convicted on gambling-related corruption charges.[9]

The people of Iowa, America's breadbasket, used to refuse to patronize any business on Sundays. Today, slot machines there operate 24 hours a day. The state has 10 major casinos. The rate of reported gambling addiction has tripled in less than six years, and nine of 10 Iowans say they patronize the industry. Attendance at the state fair has suffered as gamblers squander resources in lonely communion with gambling video screens.[10] Gambling is the weed of vices, but like all vices it has this effect: When legalized to this degree, it doesn't go away, it goes everywhere.

7. Congress must create a National Gambling Commission to put this weed and its cultural pollution under a microscope. That is the first necessary step in a process that should result in reclaiming an American ethic of hard work and fair play. Such a commission would gather and analyze the scattered but rapidly developing body of information on the impact of gambling on individuals and neighborhoods, as well as on local and state economies. Issues from the corruption of public officials to the spread of gambling addiction would be reviewed. The harm to gamblers—from accumulation of debt to elevated risk of suicide—and their families would also be studied.

Some might argue that even a fact-finding commission poses the risk of making government more intrusive, a goal the pro-family movement generally opposes. But John Kindt, a professor of commerce at the University of Illinois, has calculated that for every dollar of revenue states take in from gambling, they spend three for expanded social services and law enforcement. Thus, the gambling industry spawns the growth of government. As addiction rises and productivity losses mount, demands on government will rise even more sharply.[11]

✦ ✦ ✦

Questions for Those Who Would Lead Us

1. Will you use the moral authority of your office to speak out against cultural decay?
2. Will you refuse campaign contributions from those who are polluting our culture with gratuitous violence, exploitative gambling, and pornographic imagery?
3. Will you work to defund the National Endowments for the Arts and the Humanities to allow Americans once again to support voluntarily only those works of art and ideas they find ennobling and uplifting?
4. Will you encourage public libraries to restock their shelves with the vanishing classics of Western civilization and criticize them when they offer our children such materials as Madonna's *Sex* and *Playboy* instead?
5. Will you vigorously enforce the tough laws already on the books regarding child pornography and obscenity?
6. Will you support a national commission to study the entire issue of gambling?

✦ 10 ✦

The Green Monsters of Environmental Extremism

It isn't my line, but it's worth borrowing: The city of Washington, D.C., is largely built on what today's environmentalists would call a federally drained wetland. In the city of Boston, Fenway Park, that legendary baseball stadium with its picturesque grass and massive left-field wall (nicknamed the Green Monster), is built on swamps filled in to accommodate an expanding metropolis. Today, environmental extremists from government and academia live and play in spaces available only because previous generations of Americans were not plagued by the excesses of the contemporary movement.

Do the extremists know this? Probably. But radical environmentalism claims that it's not about forgetting the past, but about honoring and protecting our children's future. We can't, however, protect our children by scaring them to death. Above all, we can't protect them by teaching them, as we're now doing, that their greatest enemy is their fellow humanity. Conservation and stewardship of our natural resources are profoundly pro-family concepts, but environmentalism that preaches disgust at human activity has long been used to justify draconian government interference in family life.

A 1994 environmental computer program for schoolchildren from the Microsoft Corporation says it all. Under the heading "Deadliest of All," it depicts a crawling infant. "There's no denying it," the on-screen text reads, "some animals are dangerous to others. The animal shown here will grow up to be the deadliest of all—an adult human being."[1]

The hatred of humanity explicit in these words is not confined to a popular CD-ROM. Fear and hatred born of doomsday environmentalism are the messages most American children are receiving from today's textbooks and children's literature. The generation that produced the modern environmental movement and the antitechnology Unabomber is attempting to indoctrinate the next generation in its antitechnological and antiprogressive creed. As the Microsoft program makes clear, it will even glory in using technology to achieve this contradictory result.

A mother with four sons in California wrote in the *San Diego Union-Tribune* that after six weeks of kindergarten, her "once happy-go-lucky child had become a scared, worried little boy." A father wrote in the *Washington Post* about his nine-year-old daughter who, when asked to write an essay about things that bothered her, listed "lumberjacks" right after "prejudiced people" and "people who kill other people." Another parent wrote in *Audubon Magazine* that her six-year-old did not want to sleep in her wooden bed because a tree had been killed to make it.[2]

The heavy hand of government is making the nightmares of these children a reality for many adults who want nothing more than to control their own property and live in peace with both their neighbors and nature.

- ✦ In Southern California, homeowners lost their dwellings to devastating fires in 1993 when they were prevented by federal agencies from cutting firebreaks to stop the spread of brushfires. The reason: They lived in an area designated by government as protected territory for the kangaroo rat under the Endangered Species Act (ESA). The rat's habitat was worth saving, the people's was not. Ironically, the fire destroyed both—except for the house occupied by one man who broke the law.[3]

- ✦ Under the federal Superfund law, the United Truck Body Company of Duluth, Minnesota, ran up $10,000 in legal fees over eight years to protect itself against a "remedial investigation" by the Environmental Protection Agency (EPA).[4] The investigation was aimed at cleaning up a site where used motor oil was dumped. The Superfund law makes individual dumpers liable, in theory, for a total site cleanup, even if their contribution was a tiny fraction of the whole problem. One EPA bureaucrat told a small-business owner, "Don't worry, we don't want your home or car, just your business."[5]

Violations of the most basic property rights of citizens range from the ridiculous to the horrible. One elderly woman in Wyoming (population density 4.9 people per square mile) was prohibited by bureaucrats from planting a bed of roses. John Pozsgai of Pennsylvania is spending three years behind bars for cleaning up a trash dump and then adding fill dirt to mostly dry land the federal government ruled to be a wetland.[6]

Cases like these are multiplying. I haven't mentioned the well-known stories of the spotted owl and the snail darter, creatures whose protection cost many families their jobs and livelihoods. Today the EPA has broad powers, 18,000 employees, and a $4.5 billion budget. The Fifth Amendment supposedly guarantees that the national government will not take any private property for public use without "just compensation," but no provision of the Bill of Rights is more regularly flouted.

A VISION FOR A BETTER FUTURE

What would an environmentally pro-family America look like? First, the *responsible* environmentalism of the past decades would continue. Environmental awareness, linked to the concept of stewardship, is a positive development in the latter half of this century. No one wants to return to the days when choking smog enveloped places like Los Angeles; Gary, Indiana; Pittsburgh; and Detroit. The Cuyahoga River that caught fire in 1969 due to a spark from a passing train is a far cry from the clean waterway that flows through the dynamic and recovering city of Cleveland today. "Can do" environmentalism is in keeping with a long line of American thought that stretches from pioneer days to the present.

What's missing in today's radical environmentalism is balance. Book after book and tract after tract ignores the benefits derived from expanding human dominion over nature. Far from condemning technology and drafting tales of horror for children, our educated elites should tell the truth about the technological advances that have pushed back harsh frontiers, saved and lengthened lives, raised living standards the world over, and provided solutions for both natural and man-made pollution. Far from typecasting babies as the "most dangerous animal," human beings should be portrayed as the ultimate resource, the bearers of God's image, and the stewards of His creation, not its enemy.

Cleanup efforts would focus on the worst of the nation's toxic waste problems. The shotgun approach—one that hunts down small and family-owned businesses and punishes them for acts that were minimal, unforeseeable in impact, or legal at the time—would cease. Solutions would be collaborative, not combative, in all but egregious and intentional instances of pollution.

The scope of government's taking of private property would be sharply limited to cases of actual necessity, and bureaucrats and judges would enforce the compensation rights of property owners under the Fifth Amendment with the same zeal they now show in serving them notices and shoving them behind bars. Private property is the most important bulwark of all against the relentless expansion of government. Reviving the Fifth Amendment is a linchpin to keeping every other right the Constitution guarantees.

In the America we envision, businesses would wake up at last to the mistakes many have made in paying homage to the politically correct notions of entities like public broadcasting that disparage free enterprise and the family—the very forces that have been the lifeblood of our nation's prosperity. Foundations built on the fortunes of businesspeople who earned their wealth on the sweat and tears of families would no longer be turned against those families and their children.

POLICY RECOMMENDATIONS

Here are several policy steps that would constitute a responsible environmentalism:

1. Congress should reject special-interest environmentalism. The federal government's zeal for rule making has led to situations that have imposed added costs on consumers or actually fostered, rather than discouraged, environmental destruction. For example, typical "pork barrel" politics led the Clinton White House to impose a 30 percent set-aside for ethanol under alternative-fuel legislation. This small chunk of pork barrel environmentalism will cost consumers anywhere from $48 million to $350 million every year, with little or no ecological gain. And the rigid language of a 1977 amendment to the Clean Air Act favored producers of high-sulfur coal over low-sulfur producers because the latter could not as easily show the same percentage reduction in emissions.[7]

2. Modify, delay, or even repeal Corporate Average Fuel Economy (CAFE) standards. If encased asbestos had been shown to have caused as many deaths as today's CAFE standards have caused by reducing the average size, weight, and crash safety of automobile fleets, the media and Congress would have swarmed to remove every trace of asbestos from public buildings. The burden of CAFE standards, which falls disproportionately on drivers of family cars, has led to an average 500-pound reduction in vehicle weight and an extra 2,300 to 3,900 traffic deaths per year. Proposals to raise the CAFE standard to 40 miles per gallon or higher will save a little gasoline but put drivers with children ever more at the mercy of tractor-trailers and other huge vehicles.[8]

3. Modify the Endangered Species Act to protect the rights of property owners. The current structure of economic incentives under the ESA encourages property owners to destroy animal habitats or convert them to private use before federal regulators identify and mark them for preservation. This is because the discovery of such habitats denies the owners any use of those areas with no compensation in return. Changing the ESA to require compensation will convert property owners from the "enemy" into allies who can exercise public spirit and identify such habitats. If we all benefit from protection of threatened or endangered animals, all of us should bear the cost when a lawful owner suffers a loss to provide us that benefit.

4. Reject firmly—and forever—the notion of "species equality." The danger of overzealous environmentalism became obvious on a radio talk show I heard recently. The host was interviewing an animal rights activist and threw out the kind of hypothetical question I've learned not to answer. The question was, "If you were stranded at sea in a boat with a human baby and a dog, and you were running low on food and water, which of the two creatures would you throw overboard?" The activist first refused to reply. When the host persisted, she said, "That depends on whether it was *my* baby or *my* dog."

That example may be unusual, but as I pointed out above, efforts to reduce human beings to animal status—or even worse, to make them seem lower in value than animals—are all too common in today's world. For example, in a notorious editorial in the journal *Pediatrics* in 1993, Australian Peter Singer wrote, "If we compare a severely defective human infant with a nonhuman animal, a dog or a pig for example, we often find the nonhuman to have superior capacities. . . . If we can put aside the obsolete and erroneous notion of the sanctity of all human life, we may start to look at human life as it really is: the quality of life that each human being has or can achieve."[9]

Population doomsayer Paul Ehrlich has argued that "the birth of a baby in the United States, given our lifestyle support system, is 100 times the ecological disaster that the birth of a baby in Bangladesh represents."[10] His disgust with children in the developed world is so large that he has urged U.S. schools to engage in thought control. "Happy, successful families in classroom stories and films," he and his wife wrote in 1990, "should never be shown with more than two children."[11] This distorted perspective has the potential to thrust humanity into barbarism. It adds a hatred for any advanced country to a hatred for the United States.

5. Textbooks would be revised to give a balanced assessment of the impact of human activity on the planet. A school in New Jersey reacted to a challenge to a classroom book list by dropping a book aggressively promoting population control. The incident made its way into the 1995 "banned books report" from the American Library Association.[12] Too bad the local school system didn't find a way to add a pro-development book to its curriculum. There are many to choose from—and more volumes are added every month. Librarians may be unaware of the pro-development books, however, because professional publications have urged them to celebrate Earth Day with book displays that totally ignore sources expounding an optimistic view of humanity's future. This bias must end.

6. Subject environmental regulations to real-world, not remote-threat, cost-benefit analysis. Each human life is precious. No one wants to be (or should be) forced to say that government should not spend millions of dollars to save a human life from an environmental hazard. But the fact is that some environmental rules spend extremely large sums to reduce remote threats to infinitesimal levels. For public-policy makers, it may often be wiser to spend that same sum to serve a broader public interest.

In New Hampshire, for instance, a hazardous waste site was cleaned up at considerable expense to comply with federal law. But the EPA wasn't satisfied and ordered the company to spend $9.3 million more to make the site so clean that a child could safely ingest a small amount of dirt there the equivalent of 245 days a year. That would be sensible if the site were a playground, but it was actually a swamp! Might not $9.3 million have been better spent to upgrade playground equipment across the state to make it safer? As things now stand, what we do to assess risks and benefits is often skewed by environmental tunnel vision.[13]

Wise stewardship of our natural resources is a key to the better future every chapter of this book is dedicated to describing. I believe we have been given a legacy of abundance to reproduce and pass on. For all our problems, this United States of ours is still a green and growing nation. Founded on hope and thriving on opportunity, we could die on the diet of despair radical environmentalists are feeding to our precious young. Our sons and daughters need to know that the Fenway Parks of this world are not nightmares of fear but the millions of places where human activity has transformed raw nature into a field of dreams.

✦ ✦ ✦

Questions for Those Who Would Lead Us

1. Will you do everything in your power to reject the doomsaying projections of humanity's future—

especially to offer our children a vision of balanced reform, hope, and opportunity?

2. Will you work for a relaxation or even total repeal of CAFE standards that have helped to reduce production and raise the cost of the automobile models favored by families?

3. Will you work for changes in the Endangered Species Act and other environmental laws to ensure that the "taking" of private property by government regulation will be matched by full compensation of the lawful owners by the regulating agency?

4. Will you support changes to the Superfund law that will impose fair standards of liability for individuals and/or companies that engaged in minimal, nonharmful, or then-legal dumping? Will you support further changes to redirect Superfund activity from extended litigation to actual site cleanup?

5. Will you reject policy approaches that practice species equality and that refuse to favor humanity in any case of irresolvable conflict?

6. Will you support the imposition of strict cost/benefit standards that require government agencies to demonstrate reasonable returns on investment before proceeding with new regulations?

✦ 11 ✦

Pornography: Pervasive Pollution

New Yorkers, anyone will tell you, have seen it all. The residents of the Big Apple supposedly shrug their shoulders at everyday events that would appall the naive and unsophisticated. Now, however, New Yorkers seem to be saying they've seen enough. In October 1995, by a vote of 11 to 2, the New York City Council passed an ordinance that would drive out the vast majority of the sex-and-pornography businesses that have come to dominate Times Square.[1]

Times Square was once the theater capital of the United States. *42nd Street*, named after the crossing avenue where the square is located, is the quintessential musical about newcomers getting started in show biz. Theater still exists in Times Square after two decades of expanding porn and live-sex shops, with the odd result that Disney's musical *Beauty and the Beast* plays just a few feet away from Peepland's "Live Nude Girls." But Times Square, where a real revival may be just around the corner, exemplifies the inevitable result wherever pornography becomes pervasive. Times Square's 46 sex emporiums transformed a thriving cultural center with worldwide name recognition into a seedy neighborhood where residents no longer feel safe.

Times Square may be turning the corner, but the obscenity trade, with all the ingenuity of evil, is seeping through every available crack in the nation's moral foundations. In 1970, the U.S. Postal Service had identified 25 mail-order companies nationwide that engaged in the practice of sending unsolicited, sexually explicit material to homes across the country. By March 1988, there were nearly 100 such companies.[2] Sex movies now make up more than 27 percent of national video rental revenue. Rentals and sales of adult videos soared to $2.5 billion in 1994, and one analyst predicted a 15 percent increase in that figure when 1995 figures become available.[3]

Pornography is also rampant on the nearly unregulated worldwide computer system called the Internet. In June 1995, a team at Carnegie-Mellon University released the results of a quantitative analysis of over 900,000 items on the Internet. The results are nothing short of shocking. Among them:

✦ 83.5 percent of pictorial images available on Usenet newsgroups devoted to images are pornographic;

✦ 48.4 percent of all "downloads" from "adult" commercial outlets are child porn, or what clinicians call "paraphilias," which include a wide range of fetishes and perversions;

✦ the two most-frequently-accessed picture

categories on the "adult" market are child porn
and bestiality.[4]

The pervasiveness of pornography in our society has caused accelerating desensitization of otherwise sensible people. "Desensitization" is the process
by which exposure to offensive material gradually
induces a state of tolerance or indifference. In the
case of pornography users, scientific studies have
shown that desensitization actually causes individuals to "need" ever-more-graphic material to experience sexual response.[5] In the wider culture, a similar kind of tolerance leads to acceptance of ever-
expanding explicitness in the general broadcast
media. Nudity is now a commonplace not only in
evening network television broadcasts, but also in
the daytime soaps and daytime advertisements for
evening fare.

Perhaps nothing illustrates the process of desensitization better than the increasingly radical stands
taken by groups like the American Library Association (ALA). The association, which is composed of
some 3,000 library members nationwide, has insisted
on a "freedom to read" policy that makes pornography available to children in libraries on the same
basis as to adults. In the summer of 1995, library
trustees in Wellesley, Massachusetts, citing the
"Library Bill of Rights," an ALA doctrine, defended
a librarian's decision to provide a copy of *Playboy*
magazine to a nine-year-old boy. The ALA also filed
suit several years ago against a federal law requiring

pornographers to track the ages of "performers" in their films to assure that no children were being employed. The ALA chose to side with the pornographers over children, arguing that the anti-child-porn law would "chill" producers and distributors of "constitutionally protected" material.[6] The Supreme Court rejected those absurd contentions—getting an ID is routine activity when it comes to protecting minors—and upheld the law.[7]

James Malloch, whose Boston-area stores carry adult videos, says, "People's attitudes have changed. In the '70s, it [video porn] was a taboo thing.... Today people are a little more open and free."[8] That freedom has meant millions for Malloch and others in the industry. But his remarks underscore the nature of the pornography problem, which, like so many other cultural issues, is primarily a matter not of law but of the heart and soul. Laws already on the books—federal, state, and local—provide a wide variety of weapons against porn. Enforcement is often weak, but the cultural saturation of pornography involves material at the border of legality—material that, as people become acclimated to it, *pushes back* the border of legality. "Community standards" are useful only in a community where, in fact, there are standards.

In the end, pornography must never become merely an issue of how much a community will tolerate, because pornography creates a host of individual victims whose well-being is not safeguarded by the "community standard." Those harms range from the destruction of marriages to the encouragement and toleration of sexual battery and assault. Dr. Dolf Zillman of Indiana University, who has conducted research on attitudinal changes caused by "soft-core" pornography, wrote, "Whatever the specific contents of standard pornography, there can be no doubt that effects are created, and consistently so. There can be no doubt that pornography, as a form of primarily male entertainment, promotes the victimization of women in particular."[9]

A VISION FOR A BETTER FUTURE

What would an America truly intolerant of pornography look like?

In many ways, the answer is self-evident. Parents could sit and watch an evening of television with their children without having to clutch a remote control to zap entire programs or commercials that exploit sex. Travelers could pass through airport newsstands, and mothers could pass through grocery store checkout lanes, without having to shield their children's eyes from magazine covers. The mail would never bring catalogs from pornography distributors indiscriminately displaying their wares. No video store that serves families would think of offering a "room at the back" for what are absurdly called "adult" films. The sad rituals that make some men think a "stag party" is a good, old-fashioned way to celebrate on the eve of a marriage would fade into the prehistoric past to which they belong.

Feminists would close ranks behind a consistent position that recognizes the essentially moral core of the argument against pornography. The wing of feminism that values the sexual revolution and exalts the concept of "choice" over the ideals of mutual respect between the sexes would wither and die. No librarian would think that it is in any way in the public interest to purchase books like Madonna's *Sex* or *The Joy of Gay Sex* for the community. Sensitive library materials would be available to children only with the consent of their parents. Colleges would begin the year not by distributing the school "sex manual" describing various "safe sex" practices and how to obtain condoms and abortions, but by holding seminars on the health and social consequences of abandoning the marital norm.

Federal and state officials would aggressively enforce existing laws against obscenity. No government official would appear on radio programs sponsored by "shock jocks" like Howard Stern, and no official would ever honor such a person, as New Jersey Governor Christie Todd Whitman did in 1994 by erecting a plaque to Stern at a state turnpike toll plaza. No prisoner would have access to pornography. Community notice laws, like Meghan's Law in New Jersey (which requires that citizens be alerted to the presence of convicted child molesters in their communities), would be put in place everywhere. No public official would ever again appear in a parade that tolerates the kind of nudity and vulgarity that typify gay-rights marches across the country.

POLICY RECOMMENDATIONS

Stemming the tide of pornography demands a reversal of the attitudinal changes that the Mallochs of this world exploit. Even so, the law does also have a role, and there are several policy steps that can be taken to strengthen the hand of law enforcement against obscenity.

1. Develop objective, national standards for determination of obscenity. Hard-core pornography is a lucrative business. Some suggest it is a $7–10 billion-a-year enterprise.[10] We've had obscenity laws on the books for decades, yet obscenity is widely available. Why? One reason is that our obscenity laws are practically unworkable. We need federal legislation that would embody an objective standard of what is obscene, rather than the Supreme Court's subjective *Miller* standard, under which everything is presumed to be legal until proved illegal. Specifically, any pornography showing penetration clearly visible (the "PCV" standard) should be per se illegal. Material less graphic than that could be evaluated using a test employing community standards and defenses for serious value.

2. The law should require compensation for victims of pornography. Hard-core pornography precipitates and encourages sexual violation. Professor Zillman has shown that the greater the amount of pornography an individual sees, the more lenient view of pornography he or she takes. A three-year study by Dr. Edward Donnerstein at the University of

Wisconsin measured the effects of exposure to violent pornography. He found that individuals exposed to such material were more likely, compared with a control group, to underestimate the gravity of violence in a particular film, as well as to give a low estimate of the suffering undergone by a hypothetical rape victim.[11] The 1986 Attorney General's Commission on Pornography found that rapists "are fifteen times as likely as non-offenders to have had exposure to 'hard core pornography' during childhood or between six and ten years old."[12]

Accordingly, federal legislation should be enacted to permit victims of sexual violence and rape and their families to sue pornographers when it can be shown that pornography was significantly involved in the violations.

3. Obscenity should be treated as contraband. Like drugs, obscenity harms those who consume it, and its trade is harmful to society. Obscenity should be treated as contraband, and those who purchase and maintain collections of obscenity should be prosecuted. Currently, only the sale or distribution of obscenity is prosecutable.

4. Strict liability should be the legal standard for child-porn possession and distribution. In November 1994, the Supreme Court concluded in *U.S. v X-Citement Video* that prosecutors must prove that porn distributors knew their porn contained underage "performers" in order to get a child-porn conviction. But child pornography is a heinous offense against children. Feminist writer Andrea

Dworkin told the Attorney General's Commission on Pornography that perhaps as many as three-fourths of female porn performers are themselves victims of incest or child sexual abuse. Up to 40 percent of sexually abused children will become abusers as adults. Molested children experience higher levels of emotional disturbance, depression, and drug and alcohol dependency.[13]

Therefore, a strict liability standard should apply. Under this approach, if a porn distributor's videos/magazines/computer images contain children, he or she is liable regardless of whether he or she knew the performers were underage.

5. Computer networks should be family friendly. Some claim that the Information Superhighway will soon be a "global community" of which we're all members. Right now, there's no federal law to ensure that the public areas of this superhighway are safe for children. We need a comprehensive approach to computer pornography that punishes those who make sexually explicit material available to children and who use computer networks to distribute obscene material.

6. Cable porn should not be available on anything other than an opt-in basis. When families sign up with their local cable provider, they are forced to receive into their homes whatever the provider inserts in the basic cable package—including, often, sexually graphic programs. Families then must purchase and program "lock boxes" to try to keep this material away from their children's eyes. Families should not have to make such efforts to protect themselves from offensive programs they never wanted in the first place. Instead, a federal law should be passed that requires cable programmers to restrict indecent programs to channels that are available only upon request, permitting adults to "opt in" rather than forcing parents to "opt out."

7. All child porn should be made illegal: pseudo, morphed, sketched, or written. Currently, child pornography is only illegal where there's a photograph or videotape of an actual child. Child pornography, however, doesn't stop with the exploitation of the child actually pictured. It's often used as a tool in the exploitation of other children. Pseudo-child pornography (young-looking adults made to look like children), morphed child pornography (computer composition of a child picture), sketched or painted child pornography, and written stories of incest and child molestation are used to stimulate the molester, lower the defenses of the intended victim, and teach the victim about sex acts. All these forms of child pornography should be illegal, because children were likely harmed in the chain of their production, and because they are goods whose sale supports the heinous trade in our nation's most precious treasure—our children.

8. Indecency laws should be updated to include cable and satellite transmission. Because of the widespread and pervasive nature of the broadcast medium, we have laws that ban indecent programming during hours when children are likely to be in the audience.

Cable and satellite TV have become equally widespread and pervasive, and, therefore, these media should also be regulated so as to protect children.

9. Give ordinary citizens legal standing to seek injunctions against pornographers. The problem of pornography is often the result of a lack of enforcement of local laws rather than a deficiency in the laws themselves. Citizens should be given standing to petition a court to issue an injunction when pornography laws are being violated and the local prosecutor fails to act. Some counties already have these laws, which are often called "private attorney general" statutes. Ordinary citizens will always be the first line of defense against the spread of pornography.

✦ ✦ ✦

Questions for Those Who Would Lead Us

FOR LOCAL OFFICIALS

1. Will you support the adoption of strong zoning ordinances to break up the concentration of sex-related businesses and keep them away from the civil community of schools, churches, and residences?
2. Will you appoint and/or support local prosecutors committed to strong enforcement of anti-porn laws?
3. Will you use the bully pulpit of your position to speak out against the spread of cultural pollution via pornography?
4. Will you support legislation that allows ordinary citizens legal standing to seek injunctions against pornographers?

FOR STATE OFFICIALS

1. Will you support the adoption of a state "victims of pornography" statute allowing recovery in state courts for criminal assaults in which pornography played a significant role?
2. Will you support a statute requiring cable carriers to offer sexually explicit material only on an opt-in basis?
3. Will you support legislation that allows ordinary citizens statewide legal standing to seek injunctions against pornographers?

FOR FEDERAL OFFICIALS

1. Will you support an expanded definition of child pornography that includes any material aimed at the kiddie-porn market?
2. Will you support a national per se standard that makes certain depictions automatically obscene regardless of community standards?
3. Will you support anti-porn legislation to address effectively the expansion of pornography and indecency via such new technologies as the Internet, cable, and satellite broadcasting?
4. Will you support legislation that outlaws possession—and not merely sale and distribution—of illegal pornography?
5. Will you support a federal pornography victims' compensation bill?

✦ 12 ✦

A Compact with Our Fellow Americans

On the first day of the current U.S. Congress (elected in 1994), members new and old rushed forward to adopt a Contract with America. "Get it in writing" is advice that suits the American spirit. The English barons "got it in writing" in the Magna Carta. The 13 original states "got it in writing" in the Constitution. "Say what you'll do and do what you've said" are the watchwords of representative government.

Americans were right to approve the "contract" concept. It was a proper response to politicians who routinely ask voters to "read their lips" and then break their promises. A contract increases the likelihood that politicians will keep their word. And a *compact* goes beyond even the idea of a contract. It's in keeping with our Mayflower Compact, the first plan of government for the United States.

With so much focus on political and social contracts, however, Americans have too often forgotten the most important compact of all, the one "we the people" make with each other to live, work, and play by standards of fairness and reliability. This is the

143

unwritten compact of civilization, a habit of promise keeping that has broken down in modern America. This compact is broken every time a father abandons a child, a wife leaves a husband, a teacher puts personal interests ahead of the well-being of children, or an industrialist sells a sub-par product.

No Congress can resupply this compact for a society that has forsaken it. On the other hand, if we restore such a basic compact with one another, no Congress can nullify it. In this spirit, I propose the following compact with our fellow Americans under the heading "We Mutually Pledge to Each Other . . ." I do so in the belief that on the changing of hearts depends the healing of nations. All that's needed to put this compact into effect is your signature in the space you'll find at the end. Then fill out the form at the very back of this book, tear it out, and send it to us at the address indicated. If you're a public official, the compact is identical, with the addition of one last provision.

We plan to accumulate a running total of citizens who have signed the compact, and we'll share this number with the media regularly. Please indicate on the tear-out form that you consent to our using your return as part of this statistical report. Your name will be kept confidential. Upon receiving your signed form, we'll send you a framable certificate bearing the text of the compact for you to keep.

✦ ✦ ✦

"WE MUTUALLY PLEDGE TO EACH OTHER ..."

1 In our family life, we promise to remain faithful to our spouse "until death do us part." If our marriage becomes troubled, we will seek out every available resource to support and maintain our partnership, for our mutual benefit and the benefit of any children present.

2 We promise to pursue every available means to maximize the amount of time we spend with our families, recognizing our responsibilities to our spouse, our children, and our extended kin. We will work to establish good communication and conflict-resolution patterns in our families.

3 We promise to be closely involved in the education of our children. We will help them in their studies, continually monitor their academic progress, and pay particular attention to teaching them reliable standards of right and wrong.

4 We promise to raise our sons and daughters to respect and appreciate the opposite gender, to recognize the unique and irreplaceable contributions of fathers and mothers in family life, and to preserve the gift of human sexuality for marriage.

5 We promise to spread wings of protection around our children, shielding them from violent or sexually exploitative media of all kinds, whether television, film, literature, or music. Conscious of the damage done by desensitization, we will set a good example for them by avoiding such materials and by refusing to allow even legitimate media presentations to dominate family time in our household. We will also avoid drug and alcohol abuse and will encourage those around us—children, neighbors, friends—to do likewise.

6 In our work and community life, we promise to elevate a public ethic of individual merit, regardless of ethnic or national origin or political or religious belief. We will not tolerate the expression, public or private, of bigotry on any such basis. We will judge all persons we meet by the content of their character, not the color of their skin.

7 We promise to work hard to support ourselves and our families and to engage in various volunteer programs and activities that enrich our neighborhoods and communities. We will seek to protect the weaker members of our society, including the aged, the sick, the unborn, and the needy. We recognize our personal responsibility to address problems associated with poverty in our community.

8 We promise to carry out our duties as citizens: to vote in all elections, to follow and participate in the ongoing public debate, to serve on juries, to study our nation's history, and to honor the memory of those in every generation whose actions have defended and preserved our way of life. We will look for community solutions to community problems.

9 We promise to behave courteously and ethically. We will take full responsibility for our mistakes and misdeeds, not blaming others or allowing others to suffer blame for our wrongdoing. With the exception of utter mental incapacity, we will not excuse or exonerate others of responsibility for their misdeeds and the consequences thereof. We recognize the right and duty of the state to punish transgressors of the law, and we will treat those in authority with the respect befitting their office. We will restore and practice everyday signs of courtesy and respect in our neighborhoods and cities, and we will resent no courtesy offered to us by others.

10 In our personal lives, we promise to seek to honor the Creator, who made us and endowed us with such inalienable rights as life, liberty, and the pursuit of happiness. We will practice our faith daily and will gather with others to worship regularly. Without resorting to coercion or vilification, we will encourage faith, and the fruits of faith, in others.

THE PUBLIC OFFICIAL'S ADDENDUM

11 I will do everything in my capacity as a public servant, by official word and deed, to reinforce the contractual undertakings enumerated above. I will do everything in my power to ensure that public policy buttresses and supports the American people in their roles as citizens, spouses, parents, and neighbors.

Signature

If You Have Found This Book Informative . . .

If you have found this book informative and helpful as you think about the kind of nation we want to leave to our children, we encourage you to buy multiple copies to give to the following:

- ✦ family
- ✦ friends
- ✦ neighbors
- ✦ the parents of children who attend school with your kids
- ✦ co-workers
- ✦ people at your church or synagogue
- ✦ public officials

Focus on the Family books are available at special quantity discounts when purchased in bulk by corporations, organizations, churches, or groups. Special imprints, messages, and excerpts can be produced to meet your needs. For more information, write: Special Sales, Focus on the Family Publishing, 8605 Explorer Drive, Colorado Springs, CO 80920; or call (719) 531-3400 and ask for Special Sales Department.

Notes

Chapter One

1. David S. Broder, "Looking for Leadership; Voter Rage Cools, Worries Remain," *Washington Post*, 6 Nov. 1995, A1; Ronald Brownstein, "The Times Poll: Discontent Threatens Both Parties as U.S. '96 Vote Nears," *Los Angeles Times*, 5 Nov. 1995, A1.

Chapter Two

1. National Family Issues Survey, Family Research Council, Washington, D.C., Nov. 1995. Advance data reported in *Washington Watch*, Family Research Council, 27 Oct. 1995, 2.
2. Jonathan Elliott, ed., *The Debates in the Several State Conventions, on the Adoption of the Federal Constitution, as Recommended by the General Convention of Philadelphia, in 1787, 5 vols.* (Philadelphia: J.B. Lippincott, 1863), 2:537.
3. George Washington, the Farewell Address, 19 Sept. 1796, *George Washington 1732–1799: Chronology-Documents-Bibliographical Aids*, Howard F. Bremer, ed. (Dobbs Ferry, N.Y.: Oceana Publications, 1967), 75-76.

4. John Adams to Dr. Benjamin Rush, Quincy, Mass.,
   28 Aug. 1811, *The Works of John Adams, Second
   President of the United States*, ed. by Charles
   Francis Adams (Freeport, N.Y.: Books for Libraries
   Press, 1969), vol. IX, 636.

Chapter Four
1. Kathryn Wexler, "Child's Killing Shocks Even
   Gang's Turf," *Washington Post*, 19 Sept. 1995, A3.
2. Cheryl Russell, "True Crime," *American Demo-
   graphics*, Aug. 1995, 24.
3. Ibid.
4. Adam Walinsky, "The Crisis of Public Order,"
   Atlantic Monthly, July 1995, 40-41.
5. Pierre Thomas, "Arrests Soar for Violent Crime by
   Juveniles," *Washington Post*, 8 Sept. 1995, A1. This
   article quotes Attorney General Janet Reno:
   "Unless we act now to stop young people from
   choosing a life of violence and crime, the beginning
   of the 21st century could bring levels of violent
   crime to our community that far exceed what we
   have experienced"; John J. Dilulio Jr., "Why Violent
   Crime Rates Have Dropped," *Wall Street Journal*, 6
   Sept. 1995, A19; briefing by Vice President Al Gore
   and Attorney General Janet Reno, 1 Mar. 1994, U.S.
   Newswire, 7 Mar. 1994; Sergeant Michael Nichols,
   St. Louis Metropolitan Police Department's Gang
   Intelligence Section, Testimony before the Judiciary
   Subcommittee on Juvenile Justice, U.S. Senate,
   103rd Cong., 2nd sess., 9 Feb. 1994, Senate
   Judiciary/Juvenile Justice Federal Response to

Gangs; Joe Urschel, "Expert Seeks 'Classroom of Million,'" *USA Today*, 11 Apr. 1995, 1A.

6. U.S. Department of Justice, Office of Justice Programs, Bureau of Justice Statistics, "Sourcebook of Criminal Justice Statistics—1994," 1995, NCJ-154591, Table 3.1:230.

7. U.S. Department of Justice, Federal Bureau of Investigation, Uniform Crime Reports, "Crime in the United States—1993," 4 Dec. 1994, 4.

8. Curt Suplee, "Nation's Violence a 'Public Health Emergency,' AMA Says in Report," *Washington Post*, 14 June 1995, A3.

9. U.S. Rep. Dick Armey, House Republican Conference, "Crime Statistics," U.S. House of Rep., 103rd Cong., 2nd sess., Mar. 1994, n.p.

10. Andrew Peyton Thomas, *Crime and the Sacking of America: The Roots of Chaos* (Washington, D.C.: Brassey's, 1994), 8.

11. "Crime in the United States—1993," 5, 39; Walinsky, "Crisis of Public Order."

12. Walinsky, "Crisis of Public Order," 46.

13. "Crime in the United States—1993," 13; Walinsky, "Crisis of Public Order," 52.

14. U.S. Department of Justice, Office of Justice Programs, Bureau of Justice Statistics, "Survey of State Prison Inmates—1991," WCJ-136949, Mar. 1993, 11.

15. Bill Jones, California Secretary of State, Letter to the Editor, "California's 'Three Strikes' Law Has Made Big Cuts in Crime," *New York Times*, 20 Apr. 1995, A22.

16. Armey, "Crime Statistics."
17. Morgan Reynolds, "Why Does Crime Pay?" National Center for Policy Analysis, Media Backgrounder No. 123, 8 Dec. 1992.
18. "Crime in the United States—1993," 208.
19. Armey, "Crime Statistics."
20. Fox Butterfield, "Idle Hands Within the Devil's Own Playground," *New York Times*, 16 July 1995, 3.
21. Russell, "True Crime," 24.
22. American Survey, "The Waiting Game," *The Economist*, Apr. 1995, 19.
23. National Center for Policy Analysis, Media Backgrounder No. 123.
24. Ibid.
25. Cited in Wayne LaPierre, *Guns, Crime, and Freedom* (Washington, D.C.: Regnery Press, 1994), 14.
26. "Survey of State Prison Inmates—1991," 21.
27. R. Akers, "Delinquent Behavior, Drugs, and Alcohol: What Is the Relationship?" *Today's Delinquent* 3, 1984, 19–48; L.S. Wright, "High School Polydrug Users and Abusers," *Adolescence*, vol. 20, no. 80, 853–61.
28. "Preliminary Estimates from the 1994 National Household Survey on Drug Abuse," Advance Report Number 10, Substance Abuse and Mental Health Services Administration, U.S. Dept. of Health and Human Services, Sept. 1995, 3.
29. "'Precious Ground' Lost as More Youths Turn On," *Fort Lauderdale Sun-Sentinel*, 12 Dec. 1994, A1.
30. See, generally, Charmaine Crouse Yoest, ed., *Free*

to Be Family: Helping Mothers and Fathers Meet the Needs of the Next Generation of American Children, a special report from Family Research Council, Washington, D.C., 1992, 16-17, 97; and Elaine Ciulla Kamarck and William A. Galston, "Putting Children First: A Progressive Family Policy for the 1990s," Progressive Policy Institute, Washington, D.C., 27 Sept. 1990.

Chapter Five
1. "Queens Abort Butcher First Ever Nailed for Murder," *New York Post*, 12 Sept. 1995.
2. Gallup Organization, for Americans United for Life, "Abortion and Moral Beliefs—A Survey of American Opinion," 28 Feb. 1991.
3. Quoted in Dave Andrusko, "Most Americans Would Ban Vast Majority of Abortions," *National Right to Life News*, 6 Apr. 1989, 1, 9. The poll was conducted by the *Boston Globe* and appeared in the 31 March 1989 edition.
4. Roper-Starch Poll, conducted for Focus on the Family, Mar. 1994. Analysis quoted here from a memorandum to the author dated 31 May 1994 from Focus on the Family.
5. Quoted in George McKenna, "On Abortion: A Lincolnian Position," *Atlantic Monthly*, Sept. 1995, 68. The Hitchens article appeared in *The Nation*, 24 Apr. 1989, 546.
6. McKenna, op.cit., 68.
7. Ibid., 66.
8. Joseph R. Stanton, "A.D. 1995 Restatement of the

Oath of Hippocrates (circa 400 B.C.)," Value of Life Committee, Inc., Brighton, Mass.

9. "Anatomy of the Clinton Health Plan," Family Research Council, Washington, D.C., Jan. 1994, 9.

10. John C. Goodman and Gerald L. Musgrove, "Twenty Myths About National Health Insurance," National Center for Policy Analysis, NCPA Policy Report No. 128, Dallas, Dec. 1991, Executive Summary.

Chapter Six

1. Robert Rector, "Reducing the Crushing Tax Burden on America's Families," *Backgrounder*, Heritage Foundation, Washington, D.C., 7 Mar. 1994, 1.

2. David M. Wagner, "Taming the Divorce Monster—The Many Faults of No-Fault Divorce," *Family Policy*, Family Research Council, Washington, D.C., Apr. 1994, 1.

3. Elaine Ciulla Kamarck and William A. Galston, "Putting Children First: A Progressive Family Policy for the 1990s," Progressive Policy Institute, Washington, D.C., 27 Sept. 1990, 30.

4. "Consensus Possible on Family Issues if Americans Put Children First," *In Focus*, Family Research Council, Washington, D.C., Nov. 1993, 1.

5. Judith Wallerstein and Sandra Blakeslee, *Second Chances: Men, Women, and Children a Decade After Divorce* (New York: Ticknor and Fields, 1990).

6. Marlene Jennings, Connie J. Salts, and Thomas A. Smith Jr., "Attitudes Toward Marriage: Effects of Parental Conflict, Family Structure, and Gender,"

Journal of Divorce and Remarriage, vol. 17, 1992, 67-78.

7. Michele Wiener-Davis, "Couples Discovering Marriages Can Be Saved," *USA Today*, 2 Apr. 1991, A13.

8. Harry F. Rosenthal, "Better Relations with Siblings Is Kids' Top Concern," Associated Press, 10 Mar. 1987.

9. Jan Gehorsam, "Children of Divorced Parents Are More Likely to Divorce," *Atlanta Constitution and Journal*, 21 Aug. 1991, E3.

10. Margaret F. Brinig, "A Review of *Family Law and the Pursuit of Intimacy*, by Milton C. Regan, Jr.," 79 *Cornell L. Rev.*, summer 1994, 1573.

11. Patrick Buchanan, "An American Economy for Americans," *Wall Street Journal*, 5 Sept. 1995, A14.

Chapter Seven

1. Alex Kotlowitz, *There Are No Children Here* (New York: Doubleday, 1991), x.

2. Robert Coles, *The Mind's Fate: A Psychologist Looks at His Profession* (Boston: Little, Brown, 1995), 407.

3. Dr. James Dobson and Gary L. Bauer, *Children at Risk: The Battle for the Hearts and Minds of Our Kids* (Dallas: Word, 1990), 125.

4. "Dial B for Bigotry," *Washington Watch*, Family Research Council, Washington, D.C., 18 Mar. 1994, 2.

5. Charles Augustus Ballard, "Prodigal Dad," *Policy Review*, Heritage Foundation, Washington, D.C., Winter 1995, 66.

6. Gary L. Bauer, *Our Journey Home* (Dallas: Word, 1992), 40.

7. Jack Block et al., "Parental Functioning and the Home Environments in Families of Divorce," *Journal of the American Academy of Child and Adolescent Psychiatry* 27, 1988, 207-13.

8. Michael Tanner, Stephen Moore, and David Harman, "The Work vs. Welfare Trade-off—An Analysis of the Total Level of Welfare Benefits by State," Cato Institute, Policy Analysis No. 240, 19 Sept. 1995, 1.

9. George Gilder, "The Roots of Black Poverty," *Wall Street Journal*, 30 Oct. 1995, A18.

10. Eugene Steuerle and Jason Juffras, "Correcting Distortions in the Tax-Transfer System for Families with Children," *Policy Bites* 6, Urban Institute, Washington, D.C., Apr. 1991, 3.

11. John J. Miller and Stephen Moore, "A National ID System: Big Brother's Solution to Illegal Immigration," Cato Institute, Policy Analysis No. 237, 7 Sept. 1995, 4-5.

12. Stephen Moore and Dean Stansel, "Ending Corporate Welfare as We Know It," Cato Institute, Policy Analysis No. 225, 12 May 1995, 1.

Chapter Eight

1. Peter Brimelow and Leslie Spencer, "The National Extortion Association," *Forbes*, June 1993, reprint, unpaginated.

2. "Decline Found in Reading Proficiency of High School Seniors," *New York Times*, 28 Apr. 1995, A18.

3. "Violence in the Schools: How America's School Boards Are Safeguarding Your Children," National School Boards Association, Alexandria, Va., 1993, 4.

4. Ibid., 3.

5. "New Book Charges Inner-City Youth Are Schools' Chief Victims, Calls for Educational Choice," Cato Institute, July 1991, 2.

6. "The Exodus," *U.S. News & World Report*, 9 Dec. 1991, 71.

7. Jeanne Allen, "Nine Phoney Assertions About School Choice—Answering the Critics," Heritage Backgrounder No. 852, Heritage Foundation, Washington, D.C., 13 Sept. 1991, 5–6.

8. Carol Innerst, "History Test Results Aren't Encouraging," *Washington Times*, 2 Nov. 1995, A2.

9. Diane Ravitch and Chester E. Finn Jr., *Civil War: What Do Our 17-Year-Olds Know?* (New York: Harper & Row, 1987), 49.

10. See Lynne Cheney, "The End of History," *Wall Street Journal*, 20 Oct. 1994, A22; and Gary L. Bauer, former undersecretary of education, "National History Standards: Clintonites Miss the Moon," *Perspective*, Family Research Council, Washington, D.C., Mar. 1995, 2.

11. Carl Sandburg, *Abraham Lincoln: The War Years* (New York: Harcourt, Brace, 1939), vol. 2, 275.

12. "Souls 2000," *Washington Watch*, Family Research Council, Washington, D.C., 27 May 1994, 1.

13. Elizabeth McPike, "Learning to Read: Schooling's First Mission," *American Educator*, summer 1995, 3.

Published by the American Federation of Teachers.

14. From a letter signed by 40 experts on language to Dr. Robert V. Antonucci, Commissioner of Education, Commonwealth of Massachusetts, 14 July 1995, 2. The letter is on the letterhead of the Massachusetts Institute of Technology, Department of Linguistics and Philosophy.

15. Reginald M. Clark, "Homework-Focused Parenting Practices That Positively Affect Students' Achievement," *Families and Schools in a Pluralistic Society*, ed. by Nancy Feyl Cavkin (Albany: State University of New York Press, 1993), 85-105.

16. John Silber, *Straight Shooting* (New York: Harper & Row, 1989), 7.

17. Cathleen A. Cleaver, "Parental Rights—Whose Children Are They?" *Perspective*, Family Research Council, Washington, D.C., 20 Sept. 1995.

18. Anna T. Henderson and Nancy Burla, eds., *A New Generation of Evidence: The Family Is Critical to Student Achievement* (Cambridge, Mass., and Washington, D.C.: National Committee for Citizens in Education, 1994); in "The One-House Schoolroom: The Extraordinary Influence of Family Life on Student Learning," *Family Policy*, Family Research Council, Sept. 1995, 2.

19. Brimelow and Spencer, "The National Extortion Association."

Chapter Nine

1. William J. Bennett, press conference statement, New York City, 18 May 1995. The press confer-

ence was a joint event of Empower America and the National Political Caucus of Black Women, Delores Tucker, president. The press conference denounced Time-Warner and called upon its board of directors to change company policy.

2. "Canceled Bret Easton Ellis Book Bought by Vintage," Associated Press Newswire, 17 Nov. 1990.

3. See "The Library Bill of Rights," which reads in part, "A person's right to use a library should not be denied or abridged because of origin, age, background, or views." An incident involving the picture book *The Joy of Gay Sex* is reported as a book banning in the American Library Association's 1994-95 report, in Scott DeNicola, "Censorship! or Blowing Smoke?" *Citizen*, Focus on the Family, Colorado Springs, Colo., 18 Sept. 1995, 12.

4. Charles A. Donovan and William T. Spont, "Discarded Images: Selected Classics and American Libraries," Family Research Council, Washington, D.C., 18 Sept. 1995, 21.

5. Erika S. Sisam, "Bad Odds for Legalized Gambling," *Insight*, Family Research Council, Washington, D.C., Oct. 1994, 2.

6. Statement of the Honorable Frank Wolf, "National Gambling Impact and Policy Commission," 104th Cong. 1st sess., *Congressional Record* (11 Jan. 1995), vol. 141, no. 6, E86-87.

7. Peter Passell, "The False Promise of Development by Casino," *New York Times*, 12 June 1994, F5.

8. Wolf, "National Gambling Impact."
9. Ibid.
10. Dirk Johnson, "More Casinos, More Players Who Bet Until They Lose It All," *New York Times*, 25 Sept. 1995, A1.
11. Ibid.

Chapter Ten

1. "Dangerous Creatures: Explore the Endangered World of Wildlife," CD-ROM for Windows 1.0, Microsoft Home. Microsoft Corp. 1994, 0494 Part No. 55760.
2. Margaret K. Conditt, "Environmental Fears in Young Children," Fact Sheet, provided by the author, 4 Oct. 1995, to the Alabama Family Institute.
3. Ike C. Sugg, "California Fires—Losing Houses, Saving Rats," *Wall Street Journal*, 10 Nov. 1993, A20.
4. Kelly Herstad, "The EPA's Bureaucratic Hell," *Washington Times*, 3 Oct. 1995, A17.
5. Ibid.
6. Craig E. Richardson and Geoff C. Ziebart, *Strangled by Red Tape: The Heritage Foundation Collection of Regulatory Horror Stories* (Washington, D.C.: Heritage Foundation, 1995), 39.
7. Jonathan H. Adler et al., "Environmental Briefing Book for Congressional Candidates," Competitive Enterprise Institute, Washington, D.C., Aug. 1994, 17.
8. Ibid., "Automobile Fuel Economy Standards," unnumbered.

9. Peter Singer, "Commentaries: Sanctity of Life or Quality of Life," *Pediatrics* 72, July 1983, 128-29.

10. Robert C. Cowen, "More of Us, More Problems," *The Christian Science Monitor*, 17 Apr. 1990, 9.

11. Paul R. Ehrlich and Anne H. Ehrlich, *The Population Explosion* (New York: Simon & Schuster, 1990), 207.

12. Example raised by C-SPAN host Brian Lamb in 18 Sept. 1995 interview with Charles A. Donovan, senior policy adviser, Family Research Council, and Betty Turock, incoming president of the American Library Association, citing Robert P. Doyle, "Books Challenged or Banned in 1994-95," *Banned Books Resource Guide* (Chicago: American Library Association, 1995).

13. Adler et al., "Environmental Briefing Book."

Chapter Eleven

1. Dan Barry, "The Fading Neon of Times Square's Sex Shops," *New York Times*, 28 Oct. 1995, 23.

2. U.S. Department of Justice, "Sexually Oriented Advertisements and the U.S. Mails," *Obscenity Enforcement Reporter* 1, Mar./Apr. 1988, 3.

3. Richard Lorant, "Adult Videos Move Out of Back Rooms," *Bakersfield Californian*, 26 Aug. 1995, D8.

4. "Carnegie Mellon: Pervasive Porn," *Washington Watch*, Family Research Council, Washington, D.C., 15 July 1995, 2, citing *Marketing Pornography on the Information Superhighway: A Survey of 917,410 Images, Descriptions, Short Stories, and Animations Downloaded 8.5 Million Times by*

    *Consumers in Over 2,000 Cities in Forty Counties,
Provinces, and Territories,* 83 *Georgetown Law
Journal* 1849, June 1995.

5. David Alexander Scott, "How Pornography
Changes Attitudes," in *Pornography: A Human
Tragedy,* ed. by Thomas Minnery (Wheaton, Ill.:
Tyndale House, 1986).

6. Joint Brief of Appellants, American Library
Association et al., *American Library Association et
al. v Thornburgh,* U.S. Court of Appeals for the
District of Columbia Circuit, 16 Apr. 1990, 5.

7. Linda Greenhouse, *New York Times,* 27 June 1995,
D2.

8. Lorant, "Adult Videos Move Out of Back Rooms."

9. Scott, "How Pornography Changes Attitudes," 125.

10. Statement of Robert Bonner, U.S. Attorney for the
Central District of California, to the Los Angeles
County Commission on Obscenity and Pornog-
raphy, Apr. 28, 1988, in *Obscenity Enforcement
Reporter* 1, May/June 1988, 11. A publication of
the National Obscenity Enforcement Unit, U.S.
Department of Justice, Washington, D.C.

11. David Wagner, "Victims of Pornography:
Establishing a Right to Civil Damages," *Family
Policy,* Family Research Council, Washington,
D.C., July 1991, 2-3.

12. *Final Report of the Attorney General's Commission on
Pornography* (Nashville: Rutledge Hill Press, 1986).

13. "Child Abuse: America's New Plague," *Child
Protection Guide,* 3d ed. (Santa Rosa, Calif.:
Christian Action Network Foundation, 1989), 5.

Acknowledgments

Our Hopes, Our Dreams was prepared with the assistance of many individuals. On the Family Research Council staff, special thanks are due to Charles A. Donovan, senior policy adviser, who coordinated research and performed other tasks in moving the book to completion. Special thanks are also due to Robert G. Morrison, special assistant to the president; William R. Mattox, vice president for policy; Lt. Col. Robert L. Maginnis (USA, Ret.), policy analyst; Cathleen A. Cleaver, legal director; and Robert H. Knight, director of cultural studies, for their contributions. Lynne Edwards gathered research for the chapter on environmentalism. Betty Barrett, Erica Brotzman, and Beth Webb assisted in preparing the manuscript. Finally, I wish to thank Larry Weeden, book editor, and Al Janssen, director of book publishing, of Focus on the Family, for their commitment to the manuscript, their contribution to its development, and, above all, their patience.

Several organizations were particularly helpful in providing resource material and verifying other information used in this book. I wish to express my appreciation to Gary Palmer, president of the Alabama Family Institute; to the helpful staff members of the Competitive Enterprise Institute and the Heritage Foundation; and to the office of Sen. Phil Gramm of Texas (for ideas on welfare reform). The views contained in this book, of course, are solely my own, and no endorsement of them by these organizations or by any individual is implied in listing them here.

A COMPACT WITH OUR FELLOW AMERICANS:
TEAR-OUT FORM

I have signed and agree to abide by the compact described in chapter 12 of *Our Hopes, Our Dreams*:

_____
Signature

❑ I consent to the use of my return of this form in statistical reports compiled by Family Research Council to be shared with the media. I understand that my name will not be released or otherwise employed by FRC in publicity surrounding the Compact.

❑ I would like to receive a printed, framable copy of the Compact for display in my home.

PLEASE RECORD THE FOLLOWING INFORMATION:

Name _____

Address _____

City/State/Zip Code_____

Phone _____

◆ ◆ ◆

Send this completed form to:

Family Research Council
700 13th St., N.W.
Suite 500
Washington, D.C. 20005
(202) 393-2100
(202) 393-2134 (fax)
Internet address at http://www.frc.org